Room Service is Closed

Dispatches From The Front Desk

Sean Fox

Author's Notes

Before embarking on the journey that is the following pages, we need to get a couple things out of the way.

1. Some of the names/places may or may not have been changed to protect the innocent, guilty, or just to suit my mood.

2. I was an English major, which means that I studied English for long, long, long time. And with all that knowledge, my grammar still sucks. This book has been written, rewriting, edited, reedited, and grammar checked by people smarter than me. Should you come across grammatical errors, please just shoot some judgment my way and move on.

3. Get it out of your system now. Call me a bitch. If you don't want to now, read a couple pages.

*-   To everyone who said I could, and
to those who said I shouldn't*

Room Service Is Closed

Where There's Smoke

Dear Honda:

I am well aware of the fact that my payment is one or two or twelve days late. So will you please stop calling me every six minutes? It is a very inefficient use of your time. Namely because I know your phone number and have no plans on actually answering. Not even when you try to be sneaky and call me from a blocked number. Does anyone fall for that trick, by the way? Come on, it's 2006. We all know what's up.

Honda, you're good people so I am going to let you in on a little inside information. I can't give you what I don't have. It's like if you kidnapped Paris Hilton and tried to torture her into solving a simple math problem. You can't squeeze intelligence out of the mentally deficient and you can't squeeze money out of an empty bank account. By the way, I shouldn't have to explain this to you. Have you met some of the people that you give loans to?

I have a job interview lined up and, if I get the job you will be the first to know. Well, maybe not the first because I am sure the people at Popeye's will need to be notified immediately that I am on my way for celebratory biscuits.

So, with all this in mind, please stop calling me. You are basically paying someone to waste their time. If that really is the case, are you hiring? I enjoy getting absolutely nothing accomplished.

Sean

**

"I've been working in the customer service industry for the past seven years and I find that I am very much a people person." This is a blatant lie. I know it and so does my interviewer, Louise. But isn't that the main point of a job interview, to see how much smoke we can blow up each other's asses? Let's face facts. If this job was as great as she is trying to make it sound, then she wouldn't need to fill this position. And if I was such a great "people person", then I wouldn't be looking for a job.

Louise is an obnoxiously perky woman. There are times in this interview that I've wondered if she is actually a person or a robot crafted by the Hotel that has a short circuit in its chirpiness functions. If her attitude is any indication of the environment around here, then I am going to hate this job. But beggars can't be choosers.

Ever since my unjust termination from a major financial institution, my options have been limited. Let's just say that I now have a strong opinion about what should not be in your wallet. But I did learn the answer to the age old question of 'If I drop an F-bomb in the storage closet and no customers are there to hear it, will I still get fired?' Apparently, yes, having a potty mouth is grounds for dismissal.

"What do you think makes you a people person?" Louise crosses her legs and I try to listen for the faintest sound of scraping metal.

3

"I think it is because I can sense what a person wants. If they are happy, I know what will keep them happy. If they are upset, then I just have a way of knowing what I can do to make them happy." I'm trying to keep all movement in my face steady so that she doesn't see that I am fully expecting lightning to strike at any moment. That would be a bad thing. Surely, it would fry the rest of her circuits.

"That is certainly a good quality to have around here."

The key to a convincing lie is the follow through. "That's great because I always like to work in places where my best qualities will be used." The level of bullshit that I'm laying on is making me a little sick, but I maintain my composure. It would be a shame to waste the past half hour of lies due to a little nausea.

"To be honest, working in a hotel, you sometimes have to deal with guests that are irate. There are quite a few times where you could be yelled at by them. Would you have a problem working in those conditions?"

Now is probably not the time to mention that I once got written up for telling a customer to shut up and let me do my job so that she could go away. It is better to save that kind of thing until after I'm good and hired. "Angry customers are a fact of life in the service industry. I learned a long time ago not to take things they say personally. The most important thing is to make the customer happy." Now is not a good time, but the first chance I get, I need to make sure my nose hasn't grown.

4

"Well, that seems to be all the questions that I have for you. I must admit, I'm very impressed by your answers. If you don't mind waiting around for a few minutes, I'd like you to talk to the Front Office manager. I'm sure he would want to meet you."

It takes me a second to realize that I just totally bullshitted my way into a second interview. "Sure. I've got plenty of time."

Seeing as how my afternoon schedule consists of changing into my Homer Simpson pajama pants and yelling obscenities at TiVoed episodes of Grey's Anatomy, it can easily be rearranged. The only question is if my stomach can handle another round of bold faced lies. It will have to because my money is running out and my car payment is already thirteen days late. Not to mention keeping myself stocked in cigarettes and chocolate products is getting rather expensive.

I spend the next ten minutes trying to calm myself while imagining possible questions and suitable lies. The number of scenarios racing through my mind is giving me a headache. This is what I hate most about job interviews, the waiting. It is probably some form of psychological warfare that is supposed to shock the truth out of me, but I have to be stronger than that. My need for a paycheck demands it.

"Thanks for waiting around, Sean. I'm sorry it took so long to get up here. I'm Paul, the Front Office manager." Isn't it funny how, in the service industry, everyone uses first names only. It's like the second anyone decides to sell their soul to a place like this, their last name just disappears. Maybe it is supposed to depersonalize them. Easier to make them drones. (Resistance is futile.) That's just one of the observations I've made over the years. "Louise has told me a lot about you. I'm sure you're probably tired of questions, but I have a few more."

"I don't mind. I came here for a job interview, not a party. Questions are part of the package." This kind of talk is going to be the reason I don't get this job. Sarcasm has its place and time and this, most definitely, is not it.

"Well then, let's see." He picks up a piece of paper that has my half-assed résumé on it. I just sit there and nervously watch him stare at the piece of paper with the level of concentration that one usually reserves for War and Peace. This tells me that Paul will not be nearly as easy to bullshit as Louise was. He is, after all, not a robot. "It says here that you used to work in a casino. Tell me what that was like."

"It was probably the most fun job that I've ever had." This is a LOAD. I cannot believe I got those words out of my mouth with a straight face. "It was always sort of exciting to be around all those people playing slot machines."

"What didn't you like about working there?"

My boss. The hours. Working on a boat. The customers. Half of my fellow employees. That fact that I left every day with an ungodly hatred for the five dollar bill. The smell, sight, and touch of the whole place. (Though it was kind of fun to find out that I can fit $125,000 in one hand.) "My uniform. It was made out of purple polyester with gold stars stitched on the cuff and collar. It was butt ug. And it is really hard to be bright and cheerful when you are walking around looking like Barney, the Sad Dinosaur." That is a little more honesty than I am looking for. And from the look on Paul's face, I can tell that I've shocked him a little with that answer.

"I can certainly understand that." Yeah, that's hard to believe. Paul looks like he is no stranger to polyester. "I imagine that it gets very busy in a casino. How did you handle working under pressure like that?"

"I find that I do my best work when under pressure." This is not entirely a lie. I just left out the part about my tendency to blurt out expletives and to try to kill people with my eyes. "I like the fast paced environment. I always have something to do."

"That's good because it can get pretty hectic around here. We always need people who can remain calm under pressure." Now he said working under pressure, he did not mention anything about being calm. Those two things are completely different. "Now, something I'm always concerned with is an ability to work with other people. How do you rate yourself in this category?"

"Honestly, I have to rate myself very high. I find it pretty easy to work with just about anyone."

"Can you give me an example?"

Why the hell do they always want examples? Can't they just take my word for it? "Take my manager at the casino, Rick. We did not get along, like at all. When it came right down to it, we hated each other." This is a little more truth than I had intended to

7

blurt out. "I'm not exactly sure why, but there was some personal reason that he hated me so much. Anyway, this ended up with us getting into a huge screaming match in the office with his boss playing referee." Too honest. TOO HONEST. If I could slap myself without looking crazy, I would, just so I would stop talking. "But even though we never got along, we never let that show when we were on the casino floor." At least I was able to save myself with a lie because there wasn't a night that went by that I didn't tell him to get out of my sight or worse in front of a customer. But he deserved it. He was a total penis who made my life a living hell. And he always wore these ugly as shit Velcro shoes which I totally didn't get because how hard is it to tie your shoes? Especially since he was a big, giant homo so it's not like he didn't know how to bend over.

"It's good that you were able to keep your personal lives out of the workplace."

Paul's comment snaps me out of my mental tirade. "I think that is really the best way to keep from going insane. If you let your personal life interfere with your job, how are you supposed to get any work done?" I'm trying desperately to save this interview, but I think I shot myself in the foot by talking about my undying hatred for Rick. But I have to try. My bills like getting paid. And besides flirting with Paul, the only way I know of redeeming myself is by being a major kiss ass.

"Tell me about your ambitions?" My ambitions? What am I doing here? Interviewing for a job or filling out my eHarmony profile? (Maybe flirting with Paul isn't such an off the wall idea.) And exactly how ambitious do I have to be to be considered for a crappy job working at the front desk of a hotel?

"I'm going to be a writer." Maybe if I say this with enough confidence I can turn this interview around. People like confidence, right?

"If you're a writer, then I'm sure you are going to find lots of stories to tell here."

"I do tend to write about things that go on around me. And when I find a place that I can get these stories out there, I'm sure I will have no problem coming up with stuff." My first venture should be a hard hitting exposé on polyester suits in the work place, Yay or Nay. (Always nay.)

Paul clears his throat. "I'm sorry that I have to cut this short, but things are really busy here today. It was really nice meeting you. If you wait here for a minute, Louise will be right back in."

This has turned into the job interview from hell. It is more waiting than horrific questions. Maybe there is something to this psychological warfare that employers put their potential employees through. It apparently works because it forced more truth out of me than I was willing to part with. Maybe they should do a story about this on Dateline.

I do a quick scan of the room trying to find the cameras that are probably watching me. A picture of Louise and Paul splitting a tub of popcorn while they see how much they can make me squirm pops into my head. It makes me wonder what would happen if I just stood up and started doing the Macarena. Would they find it amusing or would it just put the final nail in my coffin?

Louise comes back into the room with the same exact robotic smile. Does she ever deactivate herself? "It was great meeting you, Sean. Thank you for coming down. We still have some more candidates to consider, but when we make a decision we will let you know."

"I appreciate your time." It is a last ditch effort to save myself and I know it. Unless there really is a hidden camera in the room, Louise doesn't know about my disclosure of hatred to Paul. Maybe I can still con her into thinking that I am the best person for the job.

On the way back to my car, where I'm down nine dollars for parking, it hits me. Macarena or no Macarena, I am so not getting this job.

Infiltration

Dear Lance Bass,

I think it is time that we had a talk. Through the years, I have stuck by you. Through every bad hair decision. Through every fashion abomination. Even when everyone was losing their shit over Justin, I was there for you. Now I believe that this level of devotion is more than deserving of you taking five minutes out of your busy schedule to do the whole knight in shining armor thing.

Being unemployed at the moment, I have had a great deal of time to plan our lives together. I am sure you have quite a busy life that keeps you constantly on the go and, rest assured, that will be the first thing to go. I can easily convert you to the lazy lifestyle. Imagine how it could be. The couch would be our best friend. It would give me an opportunity to teach you everything I have learned while being unemployed, like that you have to let pizza rolls cool for exactly three and a half minutes before shoveling them in your mouth or you will get burned. Or that it is possible to watch six hours of bitchy, white women on TV during the daytime.

11

And then for those times that we decided to get off the couch, we could take our place as Hollywood's new power couple. The paparazzi would totally hate us because we would stage fights and break up every other day just to get our picture in People magazine. Then we can jump on a plane and go adopt us a couple Madagascar Hissing Babies. We could be just like Angelina Jolie.

Think about how glorious it could be. But here's the thing, Lance. It will never happen unless you become a man of action. So, please, make with the white horse already.

Sean

***

My Homer Simpson pajama pants are in the wash because apparently six days in a row is too long to wear them without giving them a proper bath. Curling up on the couch, I scroll through my selection of Grey's Anatomy episodes, trying to decide which one to watch. Should I watch the one where Meredith is being a slut or the one where she is being a bigger slut? This is not at all productive, but it does provide a much needed outlet. I have a firm belief that you can blame all of life's problems on Meredith Grey, from my termination to the outbreak of vagina flashings in Hollywood. I find it comforting to have someone that I can focus all of my rage on. Besides, at this moment in time, I am under no obligation to be productive.

This has been my life since I got fired. I have now applied for approximately seven thousand jobs and only got a handful of interviews. Other banks won't touch me because apparently you have to have sales experience to process someone's deposit at a "real" bank. And spending six years studying Creative Writing doesn't give you a lot of skills needed in the work force. It is also a little disheartening to know that I am not qualified to work at a porn shop. (I'm pretty sure it was because I did not have the required drug habit or a STD.)

That doesn't mean that I haven't had a couple of offers. I know I am pretty desperate these days, but driving around in a truck full of refrigerated meat and meat by products doesn't really seem like a career move that I am willing to make. And yes, I do understand the concept of furniture repossession; I just don't think I am the man for the job. Sure, I like a good argument now and again, but it's the chances of having a gun pointed at me that I can't get past. Thanks for calling though.

And the classifieds aren't much help either. They are full of jobs that I'm not qualified for or they don't actually say what the job is. I'm just not the kind of person to call up a number to find out that it is work for a phone sex line. The problem is they never publish an ad like this: Seeking Unpleasant Person To Fill Highly Paid Position. Minimum People Skills Needed. Bad Attitude Required. I'm qualified for that. But bitter isn't raking in the cash.

But I've decided not to worry about that today. It has been six days since my interview at The Hotel and there has been no word. This is not a surprise. I haven't exactly been sitting by the phone waiting for their call. Granted, I have been sitting by the phone, but that's more because of the location of the remote control than out of hope. It is always important to be as efficient as possible.

Tomorrow I am planning on going out to apply for more jobs. If I don't get something soon, I am going to have no choice but to put in an application at McDonald's. While the prospect of getting an unlimited supply of free McNuggets is appealing, I'm afraid that I would stick my head in the deep fryer twelve minutes into my first shift. Either that or I would be immediately fired for inventing the McNugget grenade. Essentially, this is me launching

14

a handful of chicken at an ungrateful McCustomer. (I'm looking into a patent for this.)

I'm about to go into one of my patented rants because Meredith just did something ridiculously skanky when the phone rings. This displeases me because I don't like to be interrupted when I'm hating. Especially seeing as it is probably just someone calling to tell me about the joys of door to door ear wax remover kit sales. Or it is one of those ever so friendly bill collectors that have been hounding me for the past couple of weeks. Those are a little more fun. Right now I have them thinking that I'm a huge man whore because every time they call I pretend to be a different person that I am sleeping with. It's more amusing to make them think they are not getting their money because I'm busy trolling for boys than letting them know it's because I'm flat broke. I have a right as an unemployed person to fuck with bill collectors.

"Hello." I say this with a little extra attitude so that I can end this conversation as quickly as possible and get back to hating Meredith. (How else is she going to know she's a slut unless I am there to scream it at the TV?)

"Hi, Sean. This is Louise from The Hotel." The perkiness burns this early in the morning. There has got to be a remote somewhere that controls that. She's even perky when she calls to tell me that they've found that I am the worst possible candidate and I should probably consider giving up on applying for any more jobs. "I'm calling to let you know that we've decided to extend you a job offer. That is if you are still interested, of course."

Okay. It is now official. Louise is malfunctioning and her logic sensors are impaired. The only way that I am the best person for the job is if the other applicants are ex-convicts, mass murderers, or arsonists. That's got to be the only way. And while I may be a pessimist in all aspects of life, I am not stupid. "Yes, I am still very interested." I may want to tone down the desperation a little. There is still time for her circuitry to repair itself and she can come to her senses.

"That's terrific. Let me welcome you aboard as the new overnight agent for the front desk. Now, let me get you some information for your orientation."

Finally, a job that pays real money. This means that I will be able to keep my car. But first, in celebration of my infiltration of the hospitality industry, there will be chocolate.

***

Day one behind enemy lines is not going well. I have a smile plastered on my face which goes against the nature of my facial muscles. If my lips get stuck like this, I am suing someone. It is not possible to keep up this level of cheerfulness without the assistance of some mood altering drug.

I have just been attacked by a pack of overly hyper, peppy people. This does not bode well since they are also new front desk agents, meaning they are my new co-workers. It's like they are in serious danger of breaking out into a highly choreographed cheer.

16

One of them seems like he might actually be a human being. Judging from the look on his face, Philip looks like he might be contemplating a mass homicide. The rest of them are making me want to punch them in the neck.

"Welcome, everyone, I want to congratulate you on making it this far." Why is Louise making this sound like we are on the new season of American Idol? I don't think, if given the choice, anyone would actually choose to be here. We didn't win anything. "Why don't we go around the room and say a little something about ourselves?" Let's not and say we did.

"Hi. My name is Sean. I'll be working overnight front desk. I'm a writer who just graduated from college." I feel like I am in the fifth grade or at an AA meeting.

"And what made you choose to come and work for us?"

"Because I needed a paycheck and you gave me an interview."

Everyone laughs even though I am completely serious. I didn't so much as choose to work here as I am being forced to. I would love to have a job that I actually choose to go to, but the position of Lance Bass's trophy husband hasn't come available. Until then, I have to do what I have to do to get the bills paid.

The rest of the group goes around introducing themselves and giving little tidbits that will come in handy should I ever find myself on Boring People Week of Jeopardy. I have already tuned out. Every couple of seconds I raise my eyebrows to give the impression that I am fascinated. I should be happy, seeing as how I'm getting paid to listen to boring stories, but I'm not. For the past two months, I've been sitting on my ass watching TV. It's hard to make my body adjust to becoming a productive member of society again.

The day is going mind numbingly slow. I've been here for over two hours and all I've accomplished is writing my name and social security number on seven million pieces of paper. Still, I'm getting paid, but I could have done this on my couch in my sweatpants. I never thought I would be dying to do some work.

"Now we're going to take your picture for your ID badge and then we are going to get you set up with some uniforms." (Are we going to have juice and cookies too?)

I hate ID badges. Why exactly do I have to wear a badge with my picture on it? Are the guests of this hotel going to really be interested in seeing how much I've changed since the moment I sold my soul to this place? Wouldn't a simple magnetic tag with my name on it suffice?

Here's what I hate most about it though. The person taking my picture always has to use a roll of film because she can't understand that I am, in fact, smiling. I don't care if it still looks like I am scowling. It's the best my facial muscles can do.

After the horrid ordeal with the camera, Philip and I are instructed to go to Wardrobe to pick up our uniforms. This is great because it means that I can get a small break from the Peppy Pack. The second we step out the door, our grotesque smiles melt away.

"So what drug do you think everyone in that room is on?" I knew Philip would be just as disillusioned with this whole bright and shiny thing everyone has going on.

"I thought more along the lines of industry crafted robots. What do you think our chances of survival are here in Pleasantville? They don't look like they take too kindly to negative thinkers."

"That depends on how quickly we can corrupt them and bring them over to the dark side." I love Philip. He will be my new best friend. I can just see all the fun we will have hating on our coworkers.

When we get to Wardrobe, we are greeted by a most unpleasant woman named Hilda. It's nice to see that not everyone is under the influence of an overdose of happy pills. Looking at the racks of uniforms, I am not filled with hope. They are all extremely ugly. It seems that I am destined to have hideous looking work clothes. I still have night terrors about being trapped in that fashion abortion I had to wear at the casino.

Hilda drops this pile of clothes in front of us and my face drops. I had held on to a small amount of hope that my uniform would look a little less hideous. I mean, I will be working at the front desk. One would assume they wouldn't give me something so butt ug to wear. Hilda must have noticed the despair in my eyes. "What's wrong?"

"It's brown." One look at Philip and I know he is thinking the exact same thing. But Hilda doesn't seem to approve of my

19

assessment of the uniform. "Let me put it this way, Hilda. If you checked into a hotel, would you want to be helped by someone who is dressed in something the color of poo?"

Her eyes tell me that no amount of humor is going to change the color, so I might as well just shut up. Stripped of all other options, I have no choice but to inspect the offensive garments. That's when I see them. A pair of pants that a twelve year old would be lucky to squeeze into. My fat ass doesn't stand a chance. "Hilda, while I appreciate your faith in the idea that I could fit more than half a butt cheek in these pants, you are extremely wrong. I'm fat and no amount of prayer is going to get me in these." Unpleasant I can relate to, stupid I can't.

I get the feeling that Hilda doesn't find me amusing. That's okay because I'm only using this excessive level of harsh humor to keep myself from slipping into a boredom coma. Philip understands. Speaking of him, he has lost points with me. It has only taken him a grand total of eight seconds to get his uniform. And, of course, it fits because he's like a size .5. Skinny people are the devil. If he wasn't my new best friend, I'd have to hate him.

Now, armed with a name badge which I AM SMILING IN DAMMIT and a poo brown uniform, I am now an official member of The Hotel staff. God have mercy on us all.

***

It's amazing. I just spent six years studying some of the most coma inducing crap in the existence of mankind and none of it was nearly as boring as this orientation meeting. It is rather difficult to out bore eighteenth century British literature. You have to work at that.

Right now, we are learning about the history of The Hotel. Basically, it was built a really long time ago. See how fast I got that done. But, Louise has got to drag it out into a whole spiel. "We really have to appreciate the historic quality of this place." Historic is just a nice way of saying old and in desperate need of renovation. And does something that was built when hippies ruled the earth really qualify as "historic"?

"This is all part of the image we want to convey to our guests." I suddenly feel very sorry for Louise because I realize that she has to go over this same speech week after week until the end of time. "And as part of that image, our advertising department has created a new company logo for us." The slide projector throws up an image of the hotel's name. That's it. Just the name. I wonder exactly how much money went into deciding to make all the letters capitalized. "I know this looks rather simplistic, but you see the curved line crossing through the name?" We all nod our heads like the trained monkeys we now are. "That line represents the sunrise to sunset service that our guests will receive when staying with us." It takes everything in my being not to ask, 'Then does that mean since I'm working the overnight shift, I don't have to do anything?' That might overload Louise's patience protocols.

This would not be getting on my nerves nearly as much if I didn't know that it is cutting into my Price is Right time. The beauty of working the overnight shift is that you should never have to miss The Price is Right. (Oh, Bob Barker, I miss you.) This boring presentation about how the company was founded by a man with a room and a dream cannot compete with the possibility of some crazy woman forgetting to let go of the big wheel and getting sucked into the machinery. Now that's must see TV.

But instead, I'm sitting in this lecture, learning things that are of absolutely no value to me whatsoever. I find it very hard to believe that a guest is ever going to come up to me and say, 'Who is the founder of this hotel? I demand to know this information. And in what year did his dream become a reality?' I've never been a big fan of the pop quiz.

"And now we are going to watch a video on safety training." The way Louise is talking, I swear she is a heartbeat away from telling us to pull out our mats for nap time. Which would not be an altogether unwelcome suggestion.

The safety video is priceless. It's a hard hitting exposé on the hazards that we must face every day in the workplace, starring Cindy Lou, the naïve country hick turned city girl. Cindy Lou doesn't understand why she has to go to some boring safety meeting. "Back on the farm, we shucked hay all day in the hot sun and didn't care nothin' bout no safety." So she skips the meeting. (As she should have and run to the nearest salon to do something about the rat's nest on top of her head.) Everything is going fine.

22

Cindy Lou is enjoying her day until she slips and falls on some spilled coffee. She immediately dies, going straight to hell. (Seriously.) There she is faced with a creepy old man who must show her the error of her ways. Two excruciatingly painful hours later, Cindy Lou has learned about many ridiculous scenarios that aren't going to come up in my life ever. (Am I going to be doing a lot of work with industrial sized dryers down at the front desk? Really?) Everything would be all resolved except for the fact that Cindy Lou is still dead and in hell. That's a little plot point they forgot to clear up.

As horrible as this video has been, it is nothing compared to the sexual harassment video. This included a very informative scene where one guy grabs another guy's ass while he is bent over at the water fountain in a sign of male solidarity. This does not happen in the real world. And what is the response of the victim of the Vulcan Death Grip on the ass? "I'm going to tell your supervisor." Butch up, pansy boy. With the hideous tie he's wearing, it's probably the most attention he's gotten in years.

Every job I've ever worked at has had these ridiculous videos. The casino was by far the worst because everything was casino themed. "Don't touch my ass while I'm trying to count my fives." Like there was a whole lot of sexual harassment going on when everyone is covered in some garish colored polyester. My favorite was the Customer Service People's Court where sloppy employees tried to defend themselves for shoving Doritos down their throats while making change. Lesson learned: hide the fucking Doritos.

If I have to watch one more of these videos, I might lose my mind. I imagine myself going postal in the lobby. Amid the shower of bullets will be me screaming, "How's that for safety, Cindy Lou?" And, of course, I will be equipped with my very own evil laugh.

"That's all I have for you today, so you are going to get out of here early. Tomorrow you're going to be starting in your own department, but I'm sure I will see you all around the hotel." Great. Can't wait for that. Especially for the day when she malfunctions and goes into Kill All Humans mode.

I contemplate sticking around and shoving cheeseburgers down Philip's throat (The boy is going to gain weight if it kills me), but I realize that there are Roseanne reruns on TV and, if I hurry, I can catch her butchering the national anthem or something. Leaving The Hotel, I congratulate myself on surviving day two.

**

I didn't always used to be like this. There was a time when every word that came out of my mouth was not dripping with sarcasm. That was when my biggest worries were how to get a pizza from point A to point B as quickly as possible and how to make it look like I didn't completely plagiarize my analytical paper on Pamela by Samuel Richardson. (I so did. Woe for me!) I blame this change on one thing. Wal-Mart.

When I spent my days delivering pizza, my customer interaction was limited to quick pit stops, but when I gave up the glamorous life of food delivery for retail, I stepped into another world. Depending on the customer, interaction time could last up to twenty minutes. And that's if they didn't have coupons, food stamps, or want a price check on every single item. (They are listed on the shelf!)

It didn't take long for my heart to morph into cold, hard steel. My cashier line was always the fastest because I couldn't stand to look at some of the customers any longer than I had to. And if that meant bleach got mixed with raw meat, then so be it.

But, of course, I'm exaggerating. I was not nearly as bad as I like to pretend. Most days I would go in, politely nod, and not even twitch when someone shows up with an economy sized box of enemas and four cans of corn. (Actual customer.) But then there were days when I didn't think I would make it without hurting someone. One particularly nasty bitch got the farewell, "Thank you for shopping with us. You have a lovely day. And please, get hit by a car in the parking lot." That's not really the company standard.

Miraculously, I was never fired. But I did leave the job behind, swearing I would spend as little time in that store as possible. Now, this didn't work as well as I hoped. How else am I supposed to dress Wal-Mart chic without shopping at Wal-Mart? It can't be done.

Thus ended the era of retail, which led to the casino, but I've already discussed those horrors. These jobs have taught me a very valuable lesson. I am in no way, shape, or form, a people person. Customer service is the devil. But since it is the only thing that I am trained for, I have no choice but to stay in the industry. That and I give really good bullshit.

That's why I'm nervous about starting a job in a hotel. Being a cashier means that, while it may seem horrendously long, customer interaction only lasts minutes. In a hotel, this can go on for days, weeks even. I'm not sure I can contain my attitude for that long. Surely, I will get fired in record time for calling someone on their severe case of stupidity. But if there is one thing that I learned in my unemployed phase, it is that a paycheck is a very powerful thing.

And I don't want my car to be taken away by Car Protective Services. I just can't stand the thought of someone else raising my baby.

***

My official title is Night Auditor. While this title does not give me any power over my fellow employees that is not going to stop me from pretending like it does. This way I can totally act superior and laugh at the mere front desk agents' meager attempts at bossiness. That's the problem with titles. They go straight to my head.

Since I am the Night Auditor, it would make sense that I would be doing my training, you know, at night. At least it does to me.

But apparently The Hotel does not work in the same logic system as the rest of the world. That would explain why I had to wake up at the ass crack of dawn and drive on a road littered with the DMV's rejects to get to the hotel on time. What could possibly be so important that I had to get up before God? Computer training.

I thought that there could be nothing more boring than the sound of Louise's robotically monotonous voice, but I have now seen the error in my thinking. I've been sitting in the back office for three hours and I have fallen asleep four times. I am slowly working my way through seven hundred chapters of the online training. I am learning very important lessons, like how to use the mouse to click on different parts of the screen. The education requirements for getting a job at this hotel must not be very high when they set the bar so low.

My guide through this wonderful world of the front desk is Kathryn, a bright and shiny woman who has set up all these different scenarios for me to watch. I severely hope that this Kathryn person does not truly exist because I fear what I might do to her if our paths ever cross. I am going to have nightmares for the rest of my life of her picture gesturing towards me with an open palm. (Kathryn says: Pointing is bad.)

The chapter I'm on is 'Dealing With A Tough Guest'. We've gone through a thousand different scenes that all result in an inconvenience for the guest. (Kathryn: Problem is not in our vocabulary. Me: It's a big part of mine.) I've finally made it to the last one.

A lady walks up to the front desk with her three children. The children are running around and making a great deal of noise. The lady looks tired and frustrated. How would you handle this situation?

I choose answer B: Tell the woman that if she cannot control her children, she will have to step out of line until they can behave themselves. In the real world, I am well aware that this is not the correct solution, but this is computer training. Screw it.

"I'm sorry. That is not the correct answer. You should have chosen selection A: Smile politely at the guest and mention how charming her children are."

"Only if charming is the new evil." From the other side of my desk, Philip laughs. The other people in the room scowl at me like I've just defiled some ancient holy image or something. Fuck them. Philip thinks I'm funny.

"You must remember that patience is the most important thing to have. This woman looks very frustrated, so the last thing she needs is more aggravation."

"Maybe so, but she could probably use a couple of birth control pills."

"Shhh!"

I'm a little shocked, I must say. This girl, whose name I can't even force myself to remember, just librarian shushed me. Who made her front desk hall monitor? I have every right to talk back to the chipper computer program if I want. I'm about to tell her exactly where she can shove it when one of the assistant managers, Grace, comes in. I make a snap decision that it would not make a good impression for her to see me inflicting bodily harm on a fellow co-worker.

"How is everything going in here?"

I drown out the sucks ups with their "Greats" with a resounding, "I need a cigarette or I might try to strangle Kathryn through the computer screen."

"I know. She does get a little annoying sometimes." I love Grace. I can just imagine us sitting in a bar on our days off, drinking fruity drinks, and talking massive amounts of shit about people. It will be just like an episode of America's Next Top Model, except without the modeling or Tyra trying to form Miss Jay in her own image. "Why don't we take a break? You can grab some lunch or a cigarette. Just meet me back here in thirty minutes."

Since lunch consists of what I can only assume to be a collection of raw fish sticks compressed by some sort of machinery to resemble a filet, I opt to use nicotine as my main form of sustenance. The smoking "lounge" is nothing but a room with folding chairs lining a wall and a couple of fifty cent ashtrays thrown around. I shouldn't complain though. At the evil financial institution that shall not be named, the smoking lounge was my car. You call it a dingy room badly in need of a paint job, I call it progress.

This should be a very relaxing break. It will give me a chance to get my nicotine levels up from dangerously normal. But it seems that the brown noser who went all librarian on me is a smoker as well. We sit across the room from each other trying to see who can give who the bigger evil eye. I'd like to say I am winning, but she looks like she's got a good dose of crazy going on inside her. Needless to say, this does not stop me from trying to pull some Superman shit and blow my smoke all the way across the room to hit her in the face with my super breath. My life would be so much better if I had super powers.

In the end, I did win because she got bored with our little staring contest long before I did. Finally! Having two brothers who forced me into such asinine games has paid off!

Three glorious cigarettes later, my break is over. I severely do not want to go back and listen to Kathryn yammer on about the importance of customer appreciation. I consider making a mad dash for the door, but I remember that I just mailed a check for my car payment that will surely bounce if I don't get some fundage in my bank account soon. The things I'm willing to do for the love of a good car.

Back at my computer, I make a stunning realization. The computer has volume control that I can turn off. And since everything that Kathryn is saying is printed on the screen I can still learn the valuable lessons that she is trying to shove down my throat. Surely, I would rather risk getting eye cancer from reading the screen than listen to that voice anymore. I'm kind of hating on myself for not thinking of it sooner.

It doesn't take long for the rest to fall in line with the silencing of Kathryn. Even Crazy Librarian does it when she realizes how much it speeds up the process. This learning at your own pace trend that I've started has made Kathryn completely obsolete and that makes me smile.

***

I find it terribly amusing that the computer system that the whole hotel uses is called PMS. It's this crap ass system that is older than Stonehenge and about as high tech. In the week that I've been here, the damn thing has malfunctioned every night and lost track of the guest count. To me, it defeats the purpose of having a central computer system if it can't even tell you how many people are in the hotel. But I guess when you name your system after a woman's cycle, you're pretty much asking for trouble.

They've finally decided to have me start working on the graveyard shift so I can actually see what I will be spending my nights doing. I refrained from pointing out that since I will only be working graveyard, it would have been practical to have me there in the first place. Because I am all about the sucking up to the boss.

My trainer tonight is Aden and I am seconds away from sticking her in my pocket and taking her home. She is just about the most adorable thing in the whole world. It's not just that she's bitchy. It's that she does it with an Ethiopian accent. Something about a bitchy attitude in broken English makes me smile. I've already listened to her on the phone with a pissed off guest. When she told the guest to wait for the manager to come to the phone, she ended the call with, "Do you mind if I hold you?" I can only imagine the look on that person's face.

Aden has been trying to teach me how to run the night audit reports. There are only like seven hundred that I have to do. In all fairness, this is not very hard because there is a sheet of paper that walks me through the whole process. It actually tells me which buttons to press and everything. This doesn't really seem like rocket science to me, but apparently the last person who they trained, an absolute horrid specimen of human being named Autumn, couldn't master it to save her life. So that's why they hired me.

And while I'm trying to learn all of this paperwork, I'm dealing with a lobby full of people. I didn't really expect the lobby to be so jam packed at three thirty in the morning, but I've joined the staff right as we are hosting a convention of young recovering alcoholics. All of these people have decided to replace their alcohol consumption with massive intakes of caffeine and nicotine. I can definitely understand the need, but I also understand the beauty of sleep. And I really don't see the wisdom of these people having an all-nighter right next to the lobby bar. Maybe I'm just weird.

And I refuse to believe that this many people have decided to make cigarettes such a major part of their lives and not a single one of them has their own lighter. The fact that I have given out three hundred packs of matches makes these people the WORST SMOKERS EVER!

My feet started hurting about an hour ago. This does not do a lot to ease my disposition. Aden and I are both staring at the people with a certain level of hatred because we know that if they would just leave then we could sit down. That would make the night go by much faster because I wouldn't have to stop every five seconds to bitch and moan about my feet. Dr. Scholl's is the devil.

At this point, I've decided to look on the bright side. So what if the lobby is filled with a cloud of smoke so dense that even I am having a hard time breathing? Who cares if I'm contemplating chopping my feet off just to dull the pain? Because my paperwork is almost finished and I'm about to go on my break. That is until the system crashes. Damn you, PMS. Damn you straight to hell.

"Can I get a book of matches?"

BUCKETS OF HATE!

***

Aden is scheduled to train me for two weeks, but it is only the third day and I've got a pretty firm grasp on the whole paperwork extravaganza. This is mainly because I am not brain dead. So we've made an arrangement. Since she hates the reports and I hate

33

dealing with people, we split up the duties. This way we can both keep our sanity for a short period of time.

"I cannot believe you know paperwork already. I train Autumn for a month and she don't know anything. She stupid bitch."

"With an attitude like mine, I can't afford not to be good at my job."

How true that is. The Chain Smoking Posse is still here and working my nerves. I've been tempted to try coaxing them back into their rooms with the promise of free alcohol. Getting reformed alcoholics drunk is probably something the bosses would frown upon. That's the kind of thing that is going to get me fired if I don't become irreplaceable.

But after finally meeting Autumn for the first time, I know that it won't take much to be better than her. The conclusion I came to after our short encounter is that she is a big, stupid cow. If she worried more about her job than she did her weave then there would have been no need to hire me. But since she has neither the desire nor the capacity to grasp that fundamental concept, here I am.

"I don't like you." These are the first words out of her mouth to me. "You took my job."

"No, honey, they gave it to me."

Because Autumn is a cow and can't master punching numbers into a computer, the bosses have decided to give her a less challenging job. Now she can only work the slow afternoon shift so her only major task is to stand there and try to not look stupid.

34

This is a position in which she fails miserably. My personal opinion is that she should probably be put to sleep. It is the most humane option.

I finish up my paperwork and arrange it in a nice, neat stack for someone in accounting to come and whisk away. I'm not quite sure what they do with all this crap, but it is apparently very important. There must be a quota of trees that I must kill per shift. If I don't meet it there will be hell to pay. But the problem is that now that I'm finished, I have no choice but to help people.

Thankfully, Aden has gotten bored with people asking for matches and set up a box on the front desk for them to just take. This is genius because most of the guests don't actually want to talk to us. It's really a win-win situation. But this leaves me with a slight problem that I had not expected. Without guests to help and no paperwork to do, boredom sets in. And boredom for me always means trouble.

It's a good thing that there are computers set up with the internet or I would probably die. But one can check his e-mail only so many times in one night to clear out all the weird porn sites. And thanks, but I'm not really looking to get my breasts enhanced.

I surf the web for a while, finally landing on Jen Lancaster's site and devour all her archives of bitchy goodness. I get valuable life tips from it, like how to deal with problem neighbors with whom I am currently having a major issue. (Listen, Mr. Vasquez, dogs bark. It's a fact of life. I'm sorry if mine started barking and interrupted your dinner at two o'clock in the afternoon, but you will get over it. Turn down your hearing aid if you don't want to hear it.) I only wish I could be Jen Lancaster. But not in that creepy Single White Female way.

The only problem is that I finish the archives in a couple of hours. Now I'm going to have to find something else to occupy my time. This could be quite a task because that is a whole lot of hours to fill.

***

Two weeks and counting. I've managed to keep my job against the overwhelming odds of me getting fired within the first week. I get the feeling that it has less to do with me controlling my mouth and more with the fact that no one else wants to work the stupid graveyard shift. (Except for Autumn, but we've discussed that already.)

It really hasn't been too difficult. So far my job has consisted of telling loud people to shut up and wasting a lot of paper. The worst part is how quiet it can get. Being the only person in a thirty story lobby can easily drive someone insane. It wouldn't be so bad if the night manager, Tanya, would get off her butt and leave the back office. She knows damn well she is not supposed to leave me alone for so long, but chooses to spend her entire night surfing YouTube anyway. This kind of shit may have flown with Autumn, but I am so not her. I find my own brand of amusement by calling her every couple of minutes with some stupid question just to make her think I am an idiot. (If I have to stand up all night, so does she.)

But she is really the least of my problems because today I met the ultimate evil, another one of the assistant front desk managers, Doogie. (His real name is not Doogie, but that is the nickname I've branded him with because he looks like Doogie Howser in a pimp suit. It's not really the latest in fashion.) It is impossible to take this man seriously because of his hair. It's obvious that he is having a love affair with his gel bottle. And the way he slicks it back makes his whole head look like a giant ass. How exactly do you not giggle when that is staring you right in the face?

Doogie has been on vacation for the past two weeks. I think the reason no one has mentioned him is because they have been trying to enjoy a break from the tyranny of his stupidity. Our first interaction did not go very well.

"I just want to make sure that you are filing the registration cards correctly."

"Yeah. They go in alphabetical order. I learned the alphabet a long time ago. It's not exactly brain surgery."

"But accounting says they aren't being sent to them in the correct order."

"And there are sixteen other employees at the front desk. Maybe it's one of them who doesn't know the alphabet. I'm not the only one responsible for making sure those go in the right order."

"But you're the night auditor." I'm not really following his thinking. I get the feeling that not a lot of people do.

"Yeah, I'm the night auditor, but not a kindergarten teacher. If they don't know their ABC's then there isn't a whole lot I can do for them, now is there?"

He just stands there staring at me, not able to come up with anything to say. I cannot be the only person who has ever talked back to him. Not if this is the kind of stupid shit that he brings people. Alphabetized cards? Really? Shouldn't he be more concerned with the fact that gel is probably working its way to his brain?

Instead of saying anything else, he watches me while I work. I'm sure he's hoping that I will screw something up so he can immediately reprimand me. Little does he know, I am already pretty good at my job. He probably thinks that I'm just like Autumn so I will fuck something up. I might eventually, but not while he's looking. That would just be giving him more power over me than I'm willing to let him have.

His watch over me doesn't last very long because he has to go home. He would have already been gone if Tanya had gotten to work on time, but she was running late, just like every other night that I've worked with her. If she would just come in on time, I never would have had to talk to the man. He could sit in the back office and worry about registration cards all he wanted.

For some reason I get the impression that Doogie and I are not going to be the best of friends.

***

I'm bored. Aden is no longer training me and has moved to the day shift. Why anyone would want to work the day shift is beyond me. To get to work on time you actually have to be awake before the sun. Not to mention the massive amount of morons who are on the freeways that early in the morning. It's enough to send my road rage into ultra-high gear. But Aden seems to like it. So that means that I am on my own at night now.

Tanya has taken up her usual place in the back office. Tonight she is on the phone so I am forced to find some other way to amuse myself. I really hate this because it takes a lot to keep me entertained. And I don't even have the reformed alcoholic insomniacs to keep me company. I've thought about bringing a book to read during these ridiculously slow times, but I've been told that I can't do that.

"If you are looking down in a book, then you aren't looking up at the guests." Doogie has quickly gotten a promotion from minor annoyance to my arch nemesis. I tried to point out that there usually aren't any guests down in the lobby at three thirty in the morning. "Well, you never know. A guest could walk around the corner at any moment." I hate him so hard.

Contrary to what I've always heard, there is only so much you can do on the internet before you run out of things to look up. I've already made my rounds of the different websites I usually read, getting my daily dose of what people shouldn't be wearing or what

39

latest stupid thing Britney Spears has done. So I'm left with nothing to do but watch the elevators go up and down. (It's wicked boring.)

That's when the idea came to me. Why don't I start my own website? That way I can actually write some of the bitchiness that is out there in the world. I must admit I used to make fun of people who had blogs. Until I came across Jen Lancaster's website, I pretty much thought they were just an excuse for weird people to talk about their feelings because no one really cared in the first place. And I've never been a fan of big floating letters on a black screen talking about the pain that one can never feel. (Blogs don't equal free therapy.)

But mine won't be like that. I will talk about real important problems that are facing our world today. It will tackle the hard hitting issues that no one wants to talk about, forcing them to see the errors in their lives. It is going to provoke change. People will read it and elect me president of the world, followed by awarding me the Nobel Peace Prize.

Okay, not at all. I'm sure I will only use the blog to make fun of people staying at the hotel and people who piss me off in general. No one is going to read it and think anything other than I am a giant ass that is completely bitter with his life. And they would probably be right. But it will give me a public forum to declare my love for Lance Bass. Most importantly, it'll be my blog and I can write whatever the hell I want to in it.

The only problem is that I have absolutely no idea how to set up a website. When it comes to modern technology I am pretty inept. I can barely manage to navigate the internet. Sometimes if I'm lucky I can get Google to work properly, but that's only on a good day. So I can't figure out how in the world I am going to do this whole website creation and maintenance. That's really asking a whole lot from me. And that's where Myspace comes in (Not to sound dated at all). It has the handy dandy feature of a blog already built in. All I have to do is type in my bitchy ramblings and it does the rest. It's perfect. (Not really. But it will do.)

Okay. So maybe this wasn't a meeting of the minds, but it will give me something to do and requires very little effort. Seeing as I am already going to be hating on people, I might as well put some of those thoughts down. And I will finally be able to use that college degree that I paid out of my ass for.

Hell Is My Co-workers

Dear Human Resources:

I thought that I needed to write to you so that I can address some concerns that I have been having lately. It has come to my attention that your hiring practices leave a great deal to be desired. I don't know what changes you have made in your interviewing process, but I think you should know that it sucks. I understand that this is a hotel and that you aren't going to get the highest quality of applicants, but do you even meet some of the people that you hire?

I'm not trying to tell you how to do your job or anything; I just think it might be wise to not be drunk when you are conducting these interviews. That way you might have refrained from hiring the guy who thinks thirty minutes late is on time. Or the guy who smells like three day old shrimp. Or Autumn. I feel that there have been several major lapses in judgment on your part.

These people are rather annoying and that just doesn't work for me. You may want to take into consideration how I will be inconvenienced by your hiring decisions. My hostility is already at maximum. It does not need any further stress from the incompetent boobs you have decided to stick on the front desk. With this further influence from your bonehead decisions, I cannot be held responsible for what might happen.

I have included a couple of helpful suggestions that may come in handy:

> 1) Lay off the hard liquor before all interviews.
> 2) You may want to administer an IQ test to yourself. If you do not score very well, try finding another profession.
> 3) Bad shrimp smell is an immediate no-no.
> 4) If the applicant looks like he/she may have just taken a bong hit to calm down, it might be best to pass on him/her.

If you just follow this little guide, I am sure that we will not have any future problems. Honestly, I don't really believe that because I'm sure there will be other things about future employees that bug me to no end. I will be sure to forward you a letter should I have any more helpful suggestions.

Thank you for your cooperation,

Sean

***

I have a problem and it's becoming a very serious one that will have to be handled soon. I may have to go to the higher-ups for help on this one because I'm not sure they will be too thrilled with the way I handle the situation. My way calls for violence and they don't like that so much here. But that's not really good enough because they will not rectify the problem in a way that befits this heinous crime.

Two nights out of my week I am being forced to work with the most monstrous thing imaginable. It is enough for me to want to pull out what little is left of my hair. It's really not fair that I should have to work under such abominable conditions. I wouldn't wish this pain on my worst enemies. Well, maybe a couple of them.

Mallory is one of the hotel operators. She usually only works on the weekends when the regular operator, Stella (who is me in black woman form), is off. She is enough to make me dread having to come to work on a Saturday night. (Like working on Saturday isn't traumatic enough. It's not like I would go out and, you know, do something if I was off, but that's quality time that I could be spending with my bed.) It's not that Mallory is unpleasant. I could relate to it if it was just that. No. It's much worse than that. She is abnormally perky.

There is a person like Mallory in every workplace. She's the one who is happy all the time, especially on Mondays. Everyone

44

else in the office is secretly plotting ways to kill her, just to ease the pain. You are just waiting for her to burst into song like life is just a big Disney movie. This is the person who everyone wants bad things to happen to.

My main issue here is that I have made it my personal mission in life to destroy all things perky and Mallory embodies pretty much all of them. So now I am morally obligated to kill her and everything she stands for. The only problem with this plan is that, despite everything I know, I actually like her, even with all her perky ways and annoying cheerfulness at three a.m. in the damn morning. (Seriously, it's like she is happy all the time. It's not natural.)

So my killing her plan is out. I have to find a new solution to deal with this because, for some reason, the higher ups don't see a "problem" with someone being too cheery. They obviously have no idea what they are talking about. Things would be run so differently if I was in a position of power.

I've had to devise a new and improved plan. I am going to take Mallory and train her in the ways of the bitchy and bitter. It will be an exhaustive effort because I swear that this condition is the side effect of some chemical substance, I just don't have any proof. I will not give in though. Constant vigilance!

I will start my plan by doing something about that smile that is ALWAYS on her face. No one can smile that much. It's physically impossible. I'm thinking about crafting a contraption made out of tape, string, and Silly Putty that will fight her face's natural tendencies, forcing her lips to be pointed downward permanently. Then maybe I can mass produce this for the general public, helping all others with this perky co-worker problem. (Just another reason why I should be nominated for a Nobel Peace Prize.)

The next phase of the plan is going to be the hardest. The most annoying thing about Mallory is that things actually get on her nerves, namely the stupidity of the people we are paid to help. And with good reason. Some of them are just beyond assistance. But even when she complains she sounds happy. It's almost like the guest bugging her is the best thing that ever happened. That has got to go. I'm thinking about giving her homework. For a half an hour each night she will have to sit with a recorder and tape herself saying "What, bitch!" over and over again so I can monitor her progress.

For the right amount of attitude infusion, I think I'm going to sit her down and make her watch marathons of Oxygen's Bad Girl's Club and America's Next Top Model. Then, just for good measure, I might make her watch the slaughtering of a Care Bear or a Glow Worm. This should get her up to a level of bitchiness that I can stand.

I'm sure by following these simple steps and careful monitoring Mallory will be just as unpleasant to work with as I am, if not more.

And if my experiment is a success, I could totally be the next self-help guru. My book called *Turning Your Co-Worker into a Raging Bitch: A Thirty-Eight Step Process* will sweep the nation.

People will line up for miles so I can sign their asses. I would blow Dr. Phil out the damn water. Do you think I could be on Oprah?

***

The past couple of days the overnight valet guy has decided to spend his free time at the front desk. This is incredibly annoying to me because I find him to be a complete waste of a human being. I'm pretty sure Darren's only function in this world is to convert oxygen into carbon dioxide, and I'm not convinced he does a decent job at that.

Here's the thing. Working the overnight shift is not hard. When it's slow like it has been the past couple of days, the most complicated thing that I have to do is stay awake. So we have a lot of free time on our hands. I started to use my time productively. I read websites, write, or expand my vocabulary courtesy of internet word games. (Did you know that you can use ass in those games? Then why the hell can't I use fuck? It's always there.)

Alright. It's possible that I don't use my time as productively as I should. Maybe I spend a little too much time eye-sexing the cute little Mexican cleaning boy who can't speak a lick of English. (Illegals are hot.) But at least I pretend to be at work most of the time. Darren can't even muster a good pretense.

Every night he has been coming around the front desk and using the computer to surf around Myspace-esque sites looking for skanks. He's scrolling through these pictures of women who are

47

under the false impression that lace and fat rolls go together. (They don't.) I've been watching Darren as he calls these girls, trying to hook up. My question is this: Does he really think that he's going to be able to leave in the middle of his shift to get some? Yeah, like I'm going to let that happen.

In one of his finer moments, I watched him get on his cell phone trying to hook up with one skank while using the hotel phone to try to hook up with another one. I can't for the life of me understand how he was doing this. Didn't the whores hear that he was talking to someone else? I refuse to believe Darren is good enough to pull off a double hook up. Basically because he is just not cool enough about it. "What you wearing?" is a phrase I've heard entirely too often.

When he's not on the phone trolling for greasy sluts, he's having the most inappropriate conversations with Tanya. I now know more about Darren's personal life than I ever need to know about another person. Apparently when he was sixteen he had sex with his cousin. That explains so much about him. But the thing that gets me the most is that he is really proud of it. My co-workers are quality people.

Because of Darren, I have decided that there should be a company policy that certain people should have their jaws wired shut. Life would be so much better if I didn't have to hear him talk. That would also solve the problem of him introducing phrases that should never be uttered. He's enlightened us by telling us about a game he used to play when he was a kid. He calls it "stank finger".

I do not understand this concept. I don't want to understand it. (DON'T EXPLAIN IT TO ME!)

After all this, he actually has the nerve to be offended when I call him a man whore. I'm just calling it the way I see it. If you want to prowl around the internet looking for nasty hoochies, you are a man whore. Why deny it? Own it. I own my personality dysfunctions. I'm a bitch. I'm bitter. It works for me. So I don't see why he's so offended. He just needs to admit that he's a dirty, skeevy person.

It's really lucky that my job is fairly easy and this is about the worst thing I have had to deal with so far. Because if it wasn't, they are so not paying me enough not to slap him.

***

Philip and I are dangerously close to no longer being best friends. We are about to have words and not the good kind either. I'm talking full blown hair pulling, Jerry Springer words. I will not be happy until I have an entire audience on their feet, chanting "Jerry! Jerry!" while Steve tries to pull me away.

This is very hard for me because I really like Philip. That's mainly because he is one of the only competent people who work at the front desk. And he's the only one who I've ever seen frowning. (I equate this to mean that he is the only other non-robot working here.) But that does not change the fact that I want to punch him right in the neck.

49

I know I'm guilty of bitching and moaning about a lot of petty and nitpicky things, but this is different. This is a problem that has plagued the world for centuries with no end in site. I'm talking about skinny bitches complaining about how much weight they've gained.

"I'm so fat. I've got to stop eating so much." Blah blah whine whine. Is it any wonder that I shouted "Shut up, skinny bitch." He was so asking for it. He's really lucky that I didn't pull out an old cliché like, "I will sit on you." It will only be his fault for doubting the awesome power of my ass.

Skinny people are the devil. Philip can't weigh more than twenty-five pounds soaking wet. The only thing fat on him is the lip that I'm about to give him. And after that, I am going to devise a way to inject a cheeseburger directly into his bloodstream.

The thing that is pissing me off so much about this is that I have actually looked at Philip and wondered if there was actually enough room in his body for all of his internal organs. This is a clear sign of someone NOT being fat. It's just a fact of life. And the sooner he realizes this, the sooner I can stop threatening to beat him down.

This is really a problem because it takes away from the real fat people of the world. We have an actual right to bitch and moan about being fat. We don't need to see someone who wears negative sizes talking about how rotund they are. It's a shame is what it is. This is just like the little boy who cried wolf. (Well maybe not exactly.)

You know if Philip is going to sit here and complain about how he's a gigantic pile of blubber because he ate a French fry, the least he could do is wait until I can't hear him. Seriously, I will sit on him.

***

My night is not going well so far. I think I might be going to hell. Who am I kidding? I already have my rock reserved in the VIP section. But I think I might have just gotten myself an upgrade to the Super VIP Platinum section. It's the best part of hell. I am going to be right up close to the devil and in rock throwing distance of all the people I hate. My rock is totally going to be the party spot in hell. (Martinis are on me.)

My upgrade is because of a particularly nasty fight that I got into with one of my fellow co-workers. Granted it wasn't one of the front desk agents, even though, one day it will be. I've learned that there are worse (see: dumbasses, bigger) people working in this hotel. Pretty much anyone who works in the Room Service department falls under this category. But none of them are quite as stupid as Lily. She brings a whole new level of incompetence with her to work.

When I got to work, my very first phone call was from one of our special VIP guests. These are generally the worst people in the world, the kind that feel they are entitled because they have spent so many nights. (You may have a little plastic card that says you are special, but trust me you are not.) These are the last people that I want to piss off. If they have to wait for five seconds for anything, they will not only yell at you, but they will call the corporate office to tell them of the horrific inconvenience of having to be without a complimentary toothpick.

"I have been waiting for forty-five minutes for my room service order. I called at exactly 10:18. All I ordered was some cookies and milk. I don't understand what is taking so long. It's not like you have to bake the cookies yourself. I want my cookies here in five minutes or I want to speak to your manager."

Not that I'm trying to be inconsiderate to his needs, but why exactly did he call the front desk to make this complaint? Wouldn't the logical course of action be to call, oh I don't know, Room Service? Why am I being put in charge of making sure he gets his milk and cookies? And what is he, five? By the way, speaking to my manager will not do a lot of good. Tanya will probably care less than I do.

Since I am financially obligated to help this person, I make a call to Room Service and speak to Lily. "The guy in 2421 wants to know where his order is."

"I don't know. It's after eleven. Room Service is closed."

I don't understand the logic of closing Room Service at eleven o'clock. Do they really think people are just going to stop being hungry at a specific minute? While I don't understand it, there is nothing I can do. I have no power. So people just need to get over it and stop yelling at me.

"Yes, I understand that, Lily. But you were open forty two minutes ago when he placed his order. He is a VIP and really upset, so can you please just send him up his cookies and milk so he will be happy?"

I hang up the phone, assuming this will be handled so I can go back to my life. But you know what they say about assuming something. Yeah, it means Lily is an ass.

My current state of bliss only lasts five minutes because Mr. 2421 calls back. "I still don't have my order. This is ridiculous. What kind of hotel are you running here? This is completely unprofessional." I start to tune him out because nothing productive can come from listening to him. His feelings will just get hurt when he realizes that his milk and cookies are not on the top of my list of priorities. Instead, I scroll through GoFugYourself.com reading about what Courtney Love decided to crawl out of the dumpster wearing. (Courtney, your tragic fashion choices make me laugh.) "Now what are you going to do about this?"

Oh, he actually expects me to answer. Maybe I should have been listening after all. Damn you, Bai Ling for trapping me with your abomination of a dress. "Um…I'm going to…um…go up to Room Service myself and find out why they haven't sent your order up." (I have no intention of doing this, but it sounds nice.)

"You do that. I am very disappointed in the service I am receiving at this hotel."

Shit. Now I have to have two conversations with Lily in one night. Who did I piss off in a past life?

"Lily, the guy in 2421 just called back. Why hasn't his food been sent up?"

"We can't find his order."

The stupidity limit? Just reached. "I just told you what the order was. Milk and cookies. It's not hard. Throw some cookies on a plate and some milk in a glass. There you go. Order finished. Do this within in the next five minutes or the next time he calls I'm transferring the call directly to you."

This may have been a little harsh, but I don't think so. I have to talk to Lily like this or she just doesn't get it. I don't understand what is so difficult. She doesn't even have to be good like real waiters, walking and taking orders at the same time. All she has to do is sit on her rapidly spreading ass and talk to people on the phone. It's not even multitasking.

Thankfully, I do not receive another phone call from 2421, which I can only hope means that he received his milk and cookies and is now being burped or something. Now life can finally resume. That is until I see Doogie coming out of the back office and walking straight towards me. Fuck.

"I just got a call from Lily up in Room Service. She said that she didn't appreciate you talking to her with your attitude. You need to take into consideration other peoples' feelings when you talk to them. Words can hurt." Why do I suddenly feel like I am back in kindergarten and he's about to tell me to lay down for naptime?

"It is so not my fault that Lily is a moron and cannot grasp the simplest of concepts. Meanwhile, I have an angry VIP guest yelling at me because she apparently lost his order. I was a lot nicer than he would have been if I had transferred the call where it should have gone. She should really be thanking me."

"But we all have to work together to resolve issues with the guests."

"If Lily wasn't a moron there would be no guest issue to settle."

"Okay. Excluding the fact the she is a moron, you should not have spoken to her like that."

"Baby talk isn't going to really get the point across." Really. It's like the blind leading the stupid. He's not going to understand so I shouldn't even try to argue with him, but I'm going to anyway. "I know Lily is older than the pyramids and all, but that doesn't give her the right to be such a flaming cow. She's not the one who has to deal with the angry guests when she messes up. I am."

There are stories floating around the hotel about Lily that make what little is left of my hair stand on end. Everyone hates her. People have departmental meetings to plot her demise. Forced retirement has been brought up many times. But for some reason, she is still around making everybody's life miserable. Lily is the best argument I can find for old people to be shipped to the moon or put on an ice block and set adrift.

"You just need to have more respect for your fellow co-workers. We're all a family here." Is he expecting us to all join hands and sing 'I want to buy the world a Coke'? Not really going to happen. Doogie runs away from the desk before I can go into a tirade about Lily's ineptitude. He knows he would be on the losing end of the argument.

Lily making a call to Doogie is wholly unacceptable. She will not be forgiven for giving that man ammunition against me. The fact that she cannot do her job does not equate to my having an attitude. It might just mean that she's an idiot who can't follow a simple set of instructions. There's a difference.

Of course, this means war.

And if I were a mean person, I might mention that Lily is in desperate need of a new hairdo. Sticking her finger in an electrical socket is not really an effective way of styling her hair. That look only worked for Diana Ross. And Lily is no Diana Ross. So it's a good thing I'm not a mean person.

***

Jessie is one of the front desk supervisors. When Tanya is off for the night, Jessie is the one that takes her place. I don't get to work with her that much because Autumn is the one who works on my days off and Tanya absolutely refuses to work with her. The last time they did there was a screaming match that was heard on the thirtieth floor and resulted in me getting woken up at two in the morning to come to work.

But that has changed because someone finally came to his senses and fired Autumn. There was another screaming match involved in which the psycho librarian girl told her, "Shut the fuck up before I snatch that horse hair weave off your head and shove it up your monkey ass." They decided that it might be better if neither one of them worked here anymore. (Wise decision.)

I'm happy about this change because the couple of times I have worked with her, Jessie's shifts are more about getting work done and a little less YouTube-centric. Unlike Tanya, she actually will come out of the back office every once in a while, so I'm not so bored when she's around. Leaving me to my own devices is really not a wise decision. That's when I have time to plot.

Tonight is not one of those hanging out at the front desk nights. Jessie has been holed up in the back office trying to get caught up on her paperwork. The airport closed a couple hours ago because of some really bad rain and every single person who got bumped from a flight showed up to get a room. Their frustration does not give them the right to be assholes. I'm not the one who decided to close the airport, but the way they are yelling at me, you would think I did.

My cell phone starts to buzz in my pocket. I have a new text message. 'Get me a Coke and a bag of Cheetos.' I'm regretting giving Jessie my cell phone number. It was only supposed to be used in emergencies and I do not consider Cheetos an emergency. (Unless they are for Britney Spears, then just give them to the girl.) I've tried to get her to lay off the Cheetos for a while because she always makes such a mess. She tries to launch them at her mouth and never makes it. It's like the girl has no aim. Clean up is a bitch. And I always find one, hours later, after stepping on it and smashing it into the carpet. Then I'm always the one left to explain why there were Cheetos behind the front desk in the first place.

So I leave the front desk unattended to go to the café across the lobby. I should point out that I didn't even leave the front desk alone when a woman wanted me to bring her a fork at two thirty in the morning. (Fork Lady, your legs are not broken. Get it yourself.) On this little excursion I decided to pick up a Coke for myself (and a bag of chips, a Snickers, and a couple of Kit Kats) because if Jessie's getting free shit, so am I.

When I get to the back office, I find Jessie sitting there with the overnight security guard, Jack. I don't even bitch about the fact that she has someone to hang out with while all I have is Weird Fork Lady. This is because Jessie has been long flirting with this guy and I'm just waiting for the day when I walk back here and they are having some no clothes fun. But she also has a half full Coke and an unopened bag of Cheetos sitting on her desk.

"Why exactly did I have to go fetch this crap if you already have some back here?"

"Because Jack wanted some."

Hold up a minute. I didn't even bring a fork to a guest, someone that I am paid to do shit for, what made her think that I would be okay with making a food run for her little boy toy. He is not incapacitated. What if I was actually doing something important at the front desk? (I wasn't, but that doesn't alter the fact that I could have been.)

Now I've read my name badge many times. There's not a whole lot on it, just my name, my employee number, and that butt ugly picture they made me take. Nowhere on it does it say anything about being Jessie's bitch. Nor does it say anything about being required to fetch shit for Jessie's shameless flirtation partner. If Jessie really thinks there won't be some form of retaliation, then she would be wrong. It is fucking on!

I'm at the front desk when they finally decide to come out. I've had about half an hour to plot on them, trying to find the perfect revenge. It's not that I have anything against Jessie because I actually like her. But that does not change the fact that she must be punished. I am not the resident munchie fetcher, especially for Jack, who I barely tolerate.

He has himself planted on the outside of the front desk so that he can make goo goo eyes at Jessie. I'm very close to throwing up in my mouth a little. If there's anything I can't stand in this world, it is this mushy, puppy gross flirting that I am being forced to witness. Jessie knows how I am, so I don't know why she was so surprised when I yell, "Get a room" at them.

Jack just looks at me shocked. I hear him whisper, "Does he know about us?"

"Please, fool. If you were trying to keep it a secret, you suck at it." It's all part of the master plan.

59

He tries to play it off like he is not embarrassed as shit, but he sucks at that too. Now that I know I'm getting to him, I decide to throw more comments out there. "No glove. No love." "You better be careful punching your card in the company time clock." And my personal favorite, "Boom chicka wow wow."

It doesn't take long for Jack to run off into the back to get away from me. He calls from the security office to tell Jessie that he is going to Jack in the Box. It's never said but we all know it is so he can be miles away from me. He's so sensitive. Who knew that a couple of smart ass comments could make him run for the hills? (Me. That's who.)

"You are so evil, Sean. Now he's all embarrassed and it's going to take me forever to get some."

Cock blocking is so the best form of revenge. Jessie doesn't particularly care for it, but I find it immensely amusing. And that's really all that matters. I really should have my own patented evil laugh.

***

Tanya and I are having another argument. On the rare occasions that she actually gets off her butt and comes out to the front desk, we usually get into it. The sad thing is we have so many things that we can get into actual fights about that never come up. Like how I had to wait for six hours to take my break because she was on the phone with her ex. We usually fight over much more important issues.

"No. I don't think Pumkin spitting on New York was race related. I think it was more that New York was a fucking bitch who needed to be spit on."

"How can you say that?" Because I'm white and the devil apparently. "She only spit on her because she was black. The girl wouldn't have done it if New York had been white."

"Their skin color really doesn't have anything to do with the fact that Pumkin is trash."

This argument has been going on for a couple of weeks now, ever since they started playing reruns of Flavor of Love twenty-four hours a day. She is furious because I don't see the whole spitting incident as an attack on all black people across the globe. My point is that I don't really see big political happenings going on. If I wanted to watch a big racial debate, I don't think I would tune into Flavor of Love for it. I think a better choice would be Fox News, MSNBC, or even Maury. I chalked the whole thing up to skanky whores being skanky whores. This displeases Tanya greatly.

Many of our arguments go on like this. I think this is our passive aggressive way of saying that we hate each other. It's the closest that we can get without it coming to blows. Reality television gives us an outlet to release our frustrations with no physical harm. This will be the same thing that leads us to have a three week confrontation about the Grey's Anatomy 'faggot' debacle. (Please, rehab is for serious problems, like Britney's nap time, not because you called someone a bad name. That kind of just makes you a jerk.)

I think she does this so that she can say she can't be around me and actually have an excuse to go sit in the back. But little does she know that I am not about to let that happen. Yes, I may not want to have a debate over the ramifications of a white girl hocking a spitball, but it beats staring at the elevators.

The only problem is these conversations usually only deteriorate from their already fragile foundations. They lead to some other topics, like how Camille from Cycle 2 of America's Next Top Model was robbed of winning the show just because she was black.

"And her being a complete bitch had nothing to do with it." (I have dreams about making my own audition tape for ANTM, modeling myself after Camille. "I'm not here to make friiiennnds. I'm here to win!") "And your argument doesn't really work because Tyra is, you know, black."

"But she is under such pressure from the television sponsors to make the winner white that she had no choice but to cut her loose."

"Did you even watch the show? Don't you remember her going off on one of the designers about her atrocious walk? Getting kicked off the show was the least she deserved. She needed a swift kick in the ass."

"That's just like a white person."

This is usually the point where I try to put a hole in the front desk with my forehead. Whenever Tanya gets to a point in the conversation that she can't get out of, she always pulls the 'you're white you wouldn't understand' card. The way she says it makes it sound like I am personally responsible for the oppression of black people. (I was actually accused of this one time when I worked at the casino, but I was behind a cage and wearing purple polyester. You tell me who was being oppressed.) That's just a lot of weight to put on the shoulders of someone so lazy.

"Please, we are talking about cheesy reality shows. They are not exactly at the forefront on political issues. We watch them for the catfights and hair pulling, not for their depth."

"So just because they're shallow, they can't be deep?"

"Um…yeah. That's pretty much the definition of shallow."

"I can't be around you. I'm going to go finish my work in the back." I knew it was coming. At this point I'm willing to let her go so I don't have to talk to her about the societal pressures that caused that girl to drop a big log on the floor of Flava Flav's house.

Conventional Wisdom

Dear Sales Department:

I realize that conventions are a big part of our revenue here, but I am wondering if we couldn't be a little pickier about what conventions we let stay here. It's just a thought, really. Because while they do make us a great deal of money, they are highly annoying. And since I am the one who has to deal with them and not you, I suggest you listen to me or else you may find yourself working the front desk when they show up.

Here is a list of people that I would appreciate you refraining from letting stay here come convention time:

- Old ladies
- Recovering alcoholics
- Children
- Businessmen
- Foreign people

I am aware that that cuts out a great many of the conventions out there but my sanity depends on you complying. And there has to be a convention of

nice quiet people who don't bother anyone and
don't ask for all sorts of unnecessary shit, right?

    Right?

                        Thanks in advance,

                           Sean

***

Tonight has started off as a pretty good night. On my way to work, I was going to stop at the gas station to partake in my nightly ritual of a twenty ounce Cherry Coke and a pack of Hostess cupcakes. (It's the breakfast of losers.) And that's when I saw it. A big ass sign advertising gas for $1.99. I can't even remember the last time I saw a one in front of the gas price. I nearly slammed into the car that was already pumping gas to get me some. Sure, I only had to pump half a gallon because I was already on the F, but the point is I paid very little for it.

So I've been high off the cheap gas prices tonight, not even letting the guests get on my nerves. "Yes, sir, I understand that you did not enjoy the quality of your adult movie, but I'm not going to be able to take that charge off your bill because you just admitted that you watched the whole movie." (If it was so bad, why did he keep watching?) "I'm sorry that none of the scenes appealed to you, but unfortunately there was no malfunction with the movie. That would be the only reason that we could remove the charge."

This has been happening a little more than I would like it to. Our guests think that if they bitch enough about something, we are just going to give them all sorts of free shit. In a lot of cases, they are right. It's all part of that whole 'the guest must always be happy' policy that the hotel wants us to use. I'm all about that (No, I'm not.), but I think there needs to be some sort of limit. Adult programming is not one of the things I'm willing to give out

66

for free. Businessmen are just going to have to explain why they charged "Booty Bang 3" to the company credit card.

"Yes, sir, I will pass the message along. I will certainly tell my manager that we need to have a better selection of naughty movies. No, I'm writing it down right now. You have a good night, sir." Like I'm really going to pass that message along.

It's one of our slower nights, so there isn't a whole lot for me to do. My paperwork has been done for half an hour and I've already made my rounds on the internet. The elevators aren't being too active, so I can't even watch them. And I've already defaced a picture of Doogie. (It started off as just blackening out a tooth and then just morphed into a massacre. I'm thinking about having it put on a t-shirt.) All that leaves me with is staring off into the lobby bar.

The people in the bar are about as interesting as watching the elevators. Every once in a while I get to see a hooker trying to make a sale or two drunken morons doing their best to have a fight. That provides a couple minutes of entertainment, but then I'm right back where I started. We really needed to get a higher caliber of guest in this hotel. It would be so much better for my boredom levels. And that should really be the main focus of any business.

There are these two redneck business guys sitting on the couch closest to the front desk. They are part of this convention of businessmen or dipshits (I forget which) that will be staying with us the next couple of days. The rest of them will be getting here tomorrow, but these two geniuses got here a day early for absolutely no reason whatsoever.

I'm trying so hard not to listen to their conversation, but they are making it kind of hard for me with their booming voices. And it's the most inappropriate lobby chatter that I've been forced to endure. I don't think I've ever heard the term "sweater melons" used in a conversation and it not be a joke. (Sweater melons? Really?) That just makes me hate them a little more than I already do.

"I was driving down here from Dallas tonight and I passed a gas station. All I have to say is I am so glad that gas prices are going down. It's getting expensive as hell just to drive these days."

Shit. Now I have to hate on myself for having something in common with these people. I'm not supposed to be like the drunkies in the bar. That is the cornerstone on which my superiority over them is built. And it's all going to come crumbling down around me. That's enough to kill the buzz from the cheap gas and the cupcakes combined.

"I know. And it's getting hard to run my business with them that high. I mean we have a God given right to low gas prices."

The cardinal rule of working in a hotel is that you are not allowed to make fun of the guests while in earshot. The powers that be prefer that we don't make fun of the guests at all, but that is asking a lot, especially when they make comments like that. Having an uncontrollable laughing fit while the guests are sitting in front of me is definitely considered making fun. I guess I broke

68

that rule. Luckily, I saved myself by diving under the desk before the two guys could see me.

I do not consider myself to be a religious person. I can't even say that I am somewhat religious. But I do know the Ten Commandments. (Some of them anyway.) I've never heard the commandment that says, "THOU SHALT HAVE COST EFFICIENT FUEL." I can't imagine God sitting up there, fretting about how much it costs to fill up his Hummer. I would have thought that he'd be tooling around in a hybrid or something.

I may need to brush up on my history, but did they have gas powered scooters back then? Wouldn't it have been awfully hard to get down that mountain on a Moped?

***

We have a problem, a very serious one. This is apparently something that has plagued overnight front desk agents for a long time, but this is the first time that I've ever had to deal with it. They did not train me for this. I don't have the proper certification required to handle such a dilemma.

We are infested with hookers.

There is a convention of middle aged high school math teachers in town and they are all staying with us. I didn't think that they really needed to have a whole convention about the pros and cons of the quadratic equation, but apparently I am wrong. So word has gotten around that all these men are in town and the hookers came flocking through the doors.

When I walked into the office tonight Doogie told me that it is my responsibility to protect the guests from the hooker invasion. This is so not part of my job description. If the hotel doesn't want hookers peddling their wares in the lobby, then maybe someone in "management" should tell them all to leave. Why is this being passed off onto me?

And more importantly, how am I supposed to accomplish this task? I don't have a giant bottle of Eau de Pimp. Do they think I have some sort of hooker radar to alert me to their presence? Granted, I should be able to spot them, but some of them are sneaky. What am I supposed to do if one of them decides to dress all classy so that I don't know they're a hooker? And what happens when I tell one of the hoochily dressed ones to leave and it turns out to be an everyday, garden variety whore?

But then there is the whole 'the guest can have whatever they want' aspect. If one of these skeevy math teachers wants a prostitute (Just think. They could be teaching your kids.), then aren't we supposed to let him have one. I can't really stop them because once the transaction is made the hooker becomes an invited guest. And it's not my fault the horrid little trolls can't get laid without paying for it.

And there is also the issue of personal safety. If one of the hooch monkeys comes in on their own, I'm supposed to tell them to leave. Doogie has apparently never tried to come between a hooker and her money. I certainly don't want to be the one to try. I imagine myself in a flurry of hair extensions and acrylic nails. That's not how I plan to die, thank you very much.

I haven't had a whole lot of experience with hookers in my lifetime, but I've always had this image of them on the street corner waiting for a car to pull up. The reality is a lot different. And that reality just plopped her enormous fake breasts on my front desk. Literally.

"I need to get a key to Miles Border's room." She has the top three buttons on her shirt open and the fourth doesn't look like it's holding steady. Apparently she thinks flashing every millimeter of her cleavage is going to make me more inclined to help her. Yeah. That's really the wrong tree, by like a lot.

"And are you a guest in the room?"

"Well, no, we just met tonight and he asked me to meet him here. He won't be back for a little while, so I thought I would go on up and make myself more comfortable, if you know what I mean." Yuck. I know exactly what she means and that only makes me more nauseous. Especially since she has one of those voices that you can only get from chain smoking three packs a day. That and she has a weird sunburn on her breasts that makes her cleavage all leathery.

"Sure. Let me just make you a key right now. Because at this hotel we really don't give a rat's ass about security. Would you like keys to any of the other guest's rooms while I'm at it?" The saddest part about this is that it takes her a full minute to realize that I'm being sarcastic.

"But he told me to just come up to the front desk and you would give me a key."

"Then he lied to you." I'm so not about to be a feature story on Dateline. Not like this.

"Then what am I going to do?"

A great number of things. For starters, you could put away the girls. No one is really interested in seeing all the sun burnt uckyness going on there. Except for Mr. Border in 1214 it seems. Then, you could leave me alone. After that, you can go sell your goodies on the corner for all I care.

"I'm sorry. There's really nothing I can do. The only way I can issue a key is with Mr. Border present with his ID."

"That's a stupid rule."

"Not really, but okay. If you'd like to wait for him in the bar, you are more than welcome to, but that's all I can offer." See how sweet I can be when I want a bitch to go away.

"Fine. But I better be getting paid for this time I'm waiting for him." And she made it sound like such a clandestine love affair. Stupid hooker.

I wish that was the end of my night, but reality has decided to become a roller coaster and I'm just along for the ride. Across the lobby, I see a woman walk in through the main entrance. Right away I can tell she's trouble. She just has that look about her with her booty shorts and twenty inch hooker heels.

It's as she gets closer that I notice something is not quite right about her. She is rather ugly. And I don't mean that in a 'she's just homely looking for a hooker' way. I mean this bitch is UGLY. If her ears were just a little more pointed, she would be a dead ringer for Miss Piggy, right down to the synthetic blonde hair.

Have you ever had one of those moments where you look at a woman, this usually only happens with the ugly ones, and all of a sudden it hits you? This is not a woman. Now put yourself in my position and tell me you wouldn't laugh your ass off when this thing walks up to you.

I'm biting my lip so hard I taste blood. What makes this so much worse for me is that his/her/its boobs are crooked. And not by a little bit either.

"Can you tell me what room Jeffrey Marcus is staying in?"

I actually have to speak now, but if I open my mouth I'm afraid all that will come out is a massive belly laugh. And it's not just me either. Half the lobby is staring at him/her/it. "I'm sorry, but I can't give out that information. There are house phones next to the elevator. The operator will be more than happy to connect you to his room." I'm talking rather slowly so she/he/it probably thinks I'm a little off in the head.

"I'm not a hooker, just so you know." Oh, please stop. My paycheck depends on me not laughing right at this moment. He/She/It is not making it very easy on me. If you feel the need to point out that you are not a hooker, then chances are pretty good that you're a hooker. "I'm his sister and we have to go over some financial paperwork about our parents' estate." I am literally stabbing myself in the leg with my keys. The pain is not curing me of my need to laugh. I am going to lose my job because I laughed in this man/woman/thing's face. This is not how I envisioned my termination. "You see…"

"He's in room 1830." I do not care. This could be a whole Dateline sting operation and I don't care. Stone Phillips could walk around the corner right now to interrogate me. "Sean, are you in the habit of giving out room numbers to strange men dressed like Miss Piggy?" I could not give a shit. As long as it will get this man/woman/thing away from me, I'll do anything. I'll give him/her/it a key to the damn room.

"Thanks, hon."

Tanya chooses this moment to come out of the back office and sees what is standing in front of me. I do not let her have a chance to talk or turn around like she is so trying to do. I limp as fast as I can away from the front desk. There are three puncture wounds in my leg and a cigarette with my name on it. This entitles me to a good hearty laugh until I'm in tears in the parking garage.

Here's the thing. Prostitution has been around for a very long time, long before I was born. I don't think it is reasonable to expect me to rid the world if its oldest profession single handedly. It's just not going to happen. It's a hooker infestation. You can't fumigate for that.

***

The hotel is hosting a class reunion tonight. I am not at all impressed with how they turned out. The only assumption I can make is that the cool and normal people were too busy to show up. That would definitely explain the parade of losers I'm being forced to witness. It causes me physical pain to think about what these people were like when they went to George Washington High School for the Socially Inept.

The party has been going on all night and it doesn't look like it's ending anytime soon. Before he left, Philip filled me in on their progression into a drunken stupor. And isn't drunk the only way to reminisce about the time that the head cheerleader blew the captain of the baseball team in the bathroom at the prom? The way things are going tonight, we may have a repeat performance. (Ew.)

I can't imagine what it would have been like to go to school with these people. They are very, very weird. And I thought my classmates were strange. I mean we had a guy whose name we couldn't remember because everyone called him Pig Vomit. At least we didn't have the woman who thinks a diamond studded crawfish broach is a fashion statement. (Nothing says couture like a jewel encrusted crustacean.) And this means I can say their freakish weirdness is to blame for the fact that their musical selection went from Vanilla Ice to Justin Timberlake in the course of one song.

I'm actually getting my work done despite the giant bong hit of a class reunion that is going on around me. Over the last two

75

months, I've learned how to be productive even with the massive amount of distractions. It's much easier when you just tune everyone out. Though guests do tend to get pissy when they get the feeling you aren't listening.

I now see that my nice distraction ignoring night is now over because the Titanic in a party dress is coming right towards me. A million different scenarios are playing through my mind right now. None of them good. The thing that scares me the most is this woman could conceivably swallow me whole and I'm not a tiny person. I'm thinking about ducking underneath the desk to escape, but I've already been spotted. She does not look opposed to taking a bite out of the desk to hunt me down.

"I have a complaint." Of course she does. Why else would she have waddled her way up here? Just once it would be nice if someone would come to the front desk to talk. (Not really because most of these people aren't that interesting.) But no. It's always complaints, gripes, and things that I generally don't give a shit about.

"I'm sorry to hear that. How can I assist you?" It's all about masking the utter contempt in my voice.

"Well, for starters, I am very disappointed in this hotel. We decided to hold our reunion here because we were under the impression that this was a respectable place. Clearly, we were mistaken. You should really talk to your sales department and tell them to stop lying to people about how nice your hotel is. Because, honestly, this place is a shit hole. You should be ashamed of

76

yourself to work here. How can you come to work in a place like this every day and not be completely embarrassed? I wouldn't be able to show my face in public if I were you. Just look at the inside of this hotel. It's ugly. You need a paint job in here. I would think that a place as big as this could afford a better color of paint. Really, do you have no pride in your work environment? And what about the elevators? They are too far from everything. You need to make them more accessible to the ballrooms. We're all the way across the building and shouldn't have to walk so far just to get to an elevator. It's inconvenient is what it is. This place does not take their guests into consideration at all. What kind of business are you running? And I think it is a downright shame that you don't have more bathrooms in this place. You have this many people crammed into the building and not enough bathrooms for everybody. We should not have to wait in line for almost half an hour just to use the bathroom. It's ridiculous. How would you feel if you had to wait in line to pee?" I'm still trying to figure out how I became personally responsible for everything she just listed. I am neither the manager, the owner, nor the architect of the building. How is it my fault that thirty years ago, some man didn't think ahead to the possibility that a rotund woman with obvious bladder control issues would be staying here and built some more bathrooms? What's getting me the most is this woman is still talking. "You need to put yourself in our shoes to see how it feels to be treated so badly. I hope you don't honestly expect to get our business again. We can go somewhere much nicer and it will actually be worth the money that we spent. And another thing, the food is just horrible. This is not at all the quality that we expected from this place. We were lead to believe that our selection would be better than this. If I wanted this kind of food, I could go to my son's boy scout meeting." I seriously doubt that Troop 185 would be serving crab cakes at their jamboree. And, holy shit, she's still talking. "This is a total outrage. And I haven't even started on my room yet. I can't believe you have the nerve to charge people to stay in that room. You should be paying people to even walk inside. It's hideous. When I walked in, I thought I had gone back in time to the seventies. That must be the last time anyone bothered to renovate that room. Have you been inside? What am I talking about? Of course you haven't." Still talking. "That would mean that you were actually doing something customer service related and you just don't have the time to do that. You should really consider changing professions if you can't do a simple thing like inspect a room." Still talking. She's got to be some prototype version of the Energizer bunny that fuels itself on Doritos and wine coolers. Is this some sort of test to see if my head explodes? "And I find it appalling that you expect people to sleep on that old, lumpy mattress. You cannot possibly think very much of your guests if these are the accommodations that you provide. For the money that I'm paying (Forty-seven dollars!) I expect five star service. And I hate the location. You couldn't have found a better section of the city?" Now I'm to blame for downtown Houston. I'm sure it won't be long for her to get to my atrocious behavior during the Spanish

Inquisition and the Crusades. "This is a horrible place to hold a class reunion. There's nothing but big tall buildings around and half of them are parking garages. I can't even believe this place was suggested. You really have some nerve, you know that?" Apparently, I have some nerve. "It's people like you that make it hard to be a decent person these days. For every hard working, decent American human being like me in this world there are fifty lazy, heartless assholes like you. Do you know what that makes me feel like doing?" Why bother guessing when she's going to tell me anyway. "It makes me feel like moving to Canada." There's an idea. Then she would be Canada's problem. "But I'm not going to do that. If I did, then you would be winning and I'm not going to let that happen." I've actually tried to tune her out but her voice is so annoying that it is impossible to stop. Dead people are trying to cover their ears. "I can't possibly understand why you are like this. Do you enjoy doing this to people? Is this how you get your kicks? Well, we're real people and we don't deserve to be treated this way. All we wanted was to come here and enjoy our class reunion and you have ruined it. I hope you are proud of yourself." I can't even remember why she came up here in the first place. How did this progress into the complete ruin of her crappy time with her crappy friends, who probably didn't like her that much in high school anyway? And how is it my fault? I'm just standing at the damn desk. "What do you have to say for yourself?"

I try to come up with something quick to settle her down, but I can't. I can't even remember half of what she said, so it's hard to come up with something appropriate. The whole gist of the complaint is that I'm evil, right? That should be too hard to defend. Maybe if I throw a bottle of peppermint schnapps across the lobby I can run away while she runs to fetch it.

I open my mouth and prepare to speak words so brilliant and witty that this woman will have no choice but to break down into tears. This really will be my finest moment on this earth. There really should be someone here to immortalize this moment.

And then I decide no. This woman is not deserving of my beautiful words. I cannot waste my breath trying to make this woman understand that I did not design the hotel, therefore, in no way responsible for the lack of bathrooms. And I won't even mention the fact that there is a perfectly good toilet in the room that she hates so much. It's just a quick trip up the poorly placed elevators. I just close my mouth and walk away, leaving Ms. Bitchy McTalksalot to stare in awe.

It's a good thing she's drunk and won't remember this in the morning.

***

And then there are nights like this. This is the one where I'm so bored that I actually contemplate trying to fit in the back cabinet to take a nap. (I totally can. It's very peaceful in there among the office supplies.) Our occupancy is five percent. That means there are forty-nine rooms rented out. Granted that's more rooms than your average Super 8, but this isn't the Super 8. No one is calling to complain or ask for anything, and I find it very disconcerting. There is a convention of bagpipe players or some stupid shit coming in tomorrow so I should probably try to enjoy the quiet, but I'm bored.

It's so slow that I was actually able to pull a chair up to the front desk at midnight. My paperwork took me all of forty minutes with no one bothering me. Now I'm just sitting here, staring at the ceiling, and wondering if I screamed really loudly, how many of those forty-nine rooms could I manage to wake up. A thirty story lobby is prone to a lot of echoes. My vocal cords could do a lot of damage.

There isn't a whole lot for me to do tonight. It's already four in the morning and I've surfed all my websites. I've posted a blog about something stupid someone did. I do have to do some preparation for the convention tomorrow, but right now I can sit here, rocking back and forth in my chair. (Don't tell Doogie. He hates sitting apparently.) Now would be an excellent time for a cigarette break. But I can't go anywhere.

I have no idea where Tanya is. She has completely disappeared off the face of the planet. I'm betting anything she made a key to an empty room and is taking a nap. It would not be the first time. Not even close. So, I'm stuck here at the desk by some invisible leash because she feels like she needs to relive kindergarten and have nap time. And I can't leave on the off chance that someone in those forty-nine rooms has a nightmare and needs me to give them

81

some comforting words over the phone. Which is such a crock of shit because...oh wait, the phone's ringing.

"Good morning, front desk. This is Sean. How may I assist you?" We are required to use the word assist because help implies...actually I haven't a fucking clue what it implies. I'm just supposed to say it.

"Yes, I need to get a bellman up to my room to help me with my luggage."

Let me explain something. We are not a five star hotel. We are a three star hotel. There are things that a five star has that a three star doesn't because it's a measly three star. That two star difference means basically the three star is too cheap to do the things required to bump itself up. The first thing would be hiring an overnight bellman. They just expect the night auditor to do it. That's all well and good, except when the manager on duty disappears into a black hole.

"I'm sorry, but we don't have a bellman here at this time. Their shift doesn't start until five-thirty."

"What kind of a hotel doesn't have a twenty-four hour bellman?" Does anyone do a little fucking research before they book a hotel room? We clearly state everything we do and do not have.

"I'm sorry, ma'am, but this isn't a full service hotel. We do not have all the amenities that other places offer." You're more than welcome to stay at one of those next time, cow!

"Well, what about you? Why can't you come get my bags?" Not if you're going to be a bitch about it. "You're probably just too lazy to do any work." Yes, insulting me is the perfect way to get me to do your biding.

"No, ma'am, I am the only person here right now, so I can't leave the front desk." That and I'm not a fucking bellman.

"How exactly am I supposed to get my bags downstairs?"

"Prayer." Yeah, I probably shouldn't have said that. And I probably shouldn't have hung up on her after I said it. I'm just imagining her coming downstairs with a suitcase the size of Utah on her back and venom dripping from her exposed fangs.

I am going to kill Tanya whenever I find her. It's not so much that I have to deal with these people because I have to do that anyway. But if I have to face Suitcase Lady without a jolt of nicotine, there will so be hell to pay. I will not be held accountable for my actions.

Ten minutes later and there's no Tanya, no cigarette, and a creepy looking old lady walking around the corner. I peer over the desk to see her carrying the smallest suitcase in the world. Paris Hilton's dog would not fit in this suitcase. This is the monstrosity she was going to need help bringing downstairs.

"Young man, I have a complaint." I swear one day I am going to start putting a nickel in a jar every time I hear that phrase. I'll be a millionaire in a month. "There was a young lady here a few minutes ago. I spoke to her on the phone. She was very rude to me and I think that is just awful. I believe her name was Charlotte or Sharon."

"Oh yes, Sharon. We've been having some problems with her lately." This is the only thing I love about inheriting my mother's voice. I can get away with so much shit because everyone thinks I'm a woman. I've also had a variety of names. Many people think my name is Sharon, Charlotte, Shauna, and the more popular than you would think, Shanaynay. And then when you tell them that none of those people work here, they freak out. (It's funny because it's mean.) "I've sent her away for right now and apologize for any inconvenience she may have caused you."

I print up a copy of her receipt and pass it to her across the desk. Then I stand and wait as she examines every number and letter on the page. You would think, by the level of concentration these people use to look over their bill, they were actually reading Anna Karenina or some shit.

"This bill isn't right. When I booked the room this isn't the amount that I agreed to pay." I take the bill back. This is rather annoying because it happens all the time. The stupid cows up in reservations are always making bonehead mistakes.

"What was your rate supposed to be, ma'am?" I am laying on the nice super thick because of the prayer comment.

"The lady said I would be paying $120.00 for the room, but that bill says I'm paying $140.00."

I look over the bill and find her room rate. $120.00. "See, that is how much you're paying." I point out the rate to her. "It says your room cost $120.00."

"Then why is the final total $140.40? That just doesn't make sense to me."

I have to just stand there for a few minutes because I refuse to believe that this is really the problem. Working in customer service for the majority of my adult life, I have seen a great many things, but this is too much. It really can't be. Can it? "Ma'am, that's the tax."

"But that is not what I agreed to pay. I only agreed to $120.00. You can't make me pay extra."

"But it's tax. You have to pay that. It's not really negotiable. Taxes aren't set up by the hotel. That money goes to the city and the state."

"They don't do that where I'm from. It's not right that you do it here."

"Ma'am, you're from Alabama." Did she honestly think I wasn't going to pull up her address? "They most certainly do charge tax. Almost everywhere in the country does. It's implied in the price of every purchase." Why do I suddenly feel like I'm talking to a fourth grader? Has she never bought anything in her life?

"Well, I want you to take it off my bill. That was never discussed with me and you have no right to charge things to my room just because you feel like it."

85

I've really been trying to be nice to clear my conscience, but this woman just doesn't want to let me. It's tax. This is not a new invention. It has been around for many, many years. I'm sure it has gone up a little higher since the Stone Age when she was first introduced to it, but it is what it is. I can't change that.

"I'm not going to take off the taxes. Even if I could, I wouldn't. Those aren't little charges that we put on your room because we feel like it. You are required to pay tax on everything. It might suck, but it's not going to change anytime soon. If you are really that outraged, I suggest you speak to your local congressman." Maybe he will care a little more than I do, but I seriously doubt it.

"This is horrible. I have had the worst service from you people. And I will be letting your superiors know about the way I've been treated. I'm filling out a comment card right now."

NO! Anything but a comment card. How could she be so cruel? What the fuck do I care if she fills out her nasty little comment card? It's not like the managers will ever see it. The system really breaks down considering I'm the one in charge of gathering up the cards for management. I always take out the bad comments unless they're about someone that I don't like. (Helpful hint: If you are going to fill out a nasty comment card, it is better to mail the thing in later. Chances are good that no one will ever see it if you don't. Although, if you are ever going to threaten to slap a waiter with an overcooked pancake, that's a card you might want to hand deliver to the manager. Mine got posted on the wall of a Denny's.)

The woman goes on her way and her comment card promptly goes in the trash. I don't feel at all guilty about this because it was a stupid ass complaint to begin with. Okay, she may have had some legitimate concern with the whole prayer comment and that's just barely. She should be given no further attention.

I kick back in my rather uncomfortable chair and dream of ways to destroy everything Tanya stands for. She still hasn't returned and shows no signs of it anytime soon. I swear, I don't know how that girl got into a position of power in this place. My only guess is a spectacular feat of fellatio. It's the only way.

The lobby is so quiet that I'm only seconds from falling asleep. That is a big no no here, but fuck it. It's four-thirty in the morning. No one's here. And I'm sleepy. I'm going to damn well take a nap if I want to.

Don't you know that this would be the exact moment that someone walks up to the front desk? This scares the shit out of me which, in turn, sends my chair flying backwards and me tumbling to the ground. This is not my finest hour.

"I'm so sorry. I didn't mean to scare you." Aww. Little Asian Lady is so cute with her tiny little voice and precious little accent. How do you hate someone like that, even if her sudden appearance almost made me break my head? You can't.

The whole transaction is very simple. She wants to check out. I print her out a receipt. Bam! Back to some quality sitting time.

"Excuse me. I have a question." I don't know where she is from but I want to live there forever and listen to people speak with that accent. It is much better than the Southern drawl that sounds like listening to a million copies of Britney Spears. "My taxes will be refunded to me when I get to the airport, that is right?"

No. She didn't just ask that. Two people in a row, on a night where there are only forty-nine rooms, don't understand that they have to pay taxes. There's a hidden camera somewhere in this lobby. That's where Tanya's been. This is all some big practical joke. It has to be. My sanity depends on it. "No. It doesn't."

"But I'm not from this country." Her accent has just lost all its cuteness to me.

"Yes, ma'am. I understand that, but you are in this country now. And you have to pay taxes when you are here." I cannot believe I'm having to explain this again.

"But I'm not from your country. Why do I pay your taxes?"

"Because when you're in this country, you have to pay taxes. It's just the way it is, ma'am."

"But I'm not from this country."

"I think that has been clearly established, but that doesn't change the fact that you will still have to pay taxes here. If you don't understand that then there isn't a whole lot I can do to help you. But there is not a booth at the airport giving out refunds on taxes."

"But…"

I stop her before she can even say it. She is apparently from the school of thought that says if you repeat something enough times, it magically becomes an argument. But I'm going to put a stop to that right here and now.

"Have a good day, ma'am, and thank you for staying with us." My only course of action now is to ignore her. It's all I can do. If I speak to her anymore she is just going to continue with her 'not from this country' defense. And I really don't want to start an international incident.

She finally storms off, mumbling something in a language I don't understand and have no desire to learn. I'm sure it has something to do with us dirty, American pigs and I'm alright with that.

The second she walks out the door, who should come sauntering around the corner? If it isn't Tanya looking all well rested. I walk right past her without a word. She can tell just by the look on my face that it is time for me to have a cigarette. It's a good thing I stopped and bought some on my way to work. And guess what? I paid the taxes on them.

***

Now we are hosting a group of pharmaceutical salesmen. What this convention is for is beyond me. What could they possibly be talking about here? Are they having seminars on how to put a non-icky spin on the suppository? Who funds these useless conventions?

There is not a doubt in my mind that every guest in this hotel got together while they were doing the convention crap and it was decided that they were going to spend their night getting on my last nerve. Nothing anyone says will make me believe otherwise. There is no other way to explain the horrific night I've been having so far. And it's not even halfway over.

Jessie is no help whatsoever. She has declared the phones to be my domain while she deflects people coming from the bar to complain. I'm so getting the raw end of the deal here because there are tons more phone calls than there are drunken morons. And they're all hitting on her too. Whore.

"We're ready to check out now. Can you send our receipt up? We'll be out of the room by noon."

"Um, no." I'm trying to imagine why he could think that that would be kosher. "If you want to stay in the room until noon, then you need to check out at noon, not two-thirty in the morning. I can't let you stay in a room that the computer says is vacant."

"We might not have time to check out in the morning. As you can see, it's pretty late and we are going to have to get some sleep, so we might not be awake in time. Especially with all the people from our group that are going to be down there tomorrow."

"Then you are going to have to wake up five minutes earlier to give yourself time to check out. But as of right now, you haven't even been charged for tonight, so I can't check you out now or the charge won't go through at all."

90

"I don't see what the big deal is. I do this all the time at the Holiday Inn."

Here's a phrase that I have found myself saying more often than I ever thought I would. "This is not the Holiday Inn."

The only response I get is a phone being slammed in my ear. This only stops me from having to speak to the dumbass anymore, so I'm really the winner here.

But this is not the end of my adventures with these people. Who knew that the exciting world of pharmaceutical sales was a one way ticket to the land of the stupid? And I hate them all because the damn phone will not stop ringing.

"Yeeeeesh, we's wants you to oooooooppen ze pooool. We wantses to swimming." As if it's some sort of fucked up punctuation mark for her sentence, she burps directly into the phone. All I can do is calmly repeat to myself that this bitch did not just burp in my ear. Obviously, repeating a mantra is not going to change the past.

"No, the pool is closed."

"Buts we're are gueshtes here. We's sayses it open. I was shtold the gueshtes always right."

I feel like I'm getting drunk just listening to her. "You were lied to. In most cases on record, the guest is emphatically wrong. And I won't open the pool because you're drunk and I really don't feel like being responsible should you die."

"I WANT THE FUCKING POOL OPEN RIGHT NOW, GODDAMMIT!" How she managed to not slur a single one of those words is beyond me.

"Congratulations for you. There's a lot of shit that I want that's never going to happen. So get over it." I hear her screaming something incoherent as I'm slamming the phone down. I do not have time for a drunk bitch who has clearly been dipping into all those free samples the drug companies have sent these people.

Jessie's giving me her most evil look, which she saves for when I've done something wrong. She can just shove it up her hoo haa because she could totally be helping with some of these phone calls, but she's too busy talking to the weird looking man with the crooked mustache. Slut.

I give a small shudder as I pick up the next call. "Good morning, front desk. This is Sean. How may I assist you?" Please, on everything that I hold beautiful in this world (Lance Bass's butt), let it be someone wanting a set of towels.

"Me and my wife are planning on checking out in about an hour. We're going to grab an early breakfast down at the IHOP. Maybe we'll drive around for a little while, looking at the city while the sun is coming up." Is he calling me just to give me his itinerary for the day? Because I really don't care. "We just wanted to let you know that we will be leaving our bags in the room while we're out for a bit and swing back later this afternoon to pick them up."

"Okay. But I can't check you out if you plan on leaving your stuff in the room."

"Why not?"

"Because, sir, when you check out that means that you are vacating the room. If you leave your stuff behind then that means you are still there. You can't check out until you are officially ready to leave, bags and all." Am I really the only who sees how this works?

"But we don't want to take our bags with us."

"Then leave them here. But you have to be back before noon to pick them up and to check out."

"I just don't see what the big deal is about leaving our bags here. Aren't you supposed to be trying to accommodate us? We are paying your salary." That's the beautiful thing about working the overnight shift. That argument right there does not fly. Seeing as how no one in their right mind wants to work this fucked up shift, I always have work. I get paid whether these people are here or not. So suck on that.

"Here's the thing, sir. If you check out and your bags are still in your room, our housekeepers are going to take them because they think they have been abandoned. And since most of the housekeeping staff here speaks exactly no English, it will take hours to locate your bags. Then you will be stuck here waiting for bags that you would have been better off taking with you in the first place."

"But…"

"Thank you and have a nice night." I always find saying that before hanging up on somebody eases some tension. Like people are really out there going, "He hung up on me, but at least he wished me a good night before he did it." But in my warped little mind it makes a difference.

If only the phone would stop ringing. Do none of these people sleep at night? Is this whole convention a cover up for the fact that we are hosting a convention of vampires and I just wasn't informed? Leave me alone or I will throw garlic bread at you!

"Front desk." Notice my subtle lack of hospitality in my new phone greeting. And just to make myself a little bitchier, I pick up one of the many other ringing lines and hold the receiver directly to Jessie's ear so she has no choice but to leave the confines of her whoredom and help me with these awful people.

"Yeah. I'm checking out in the morning and I've just been going over my bill. There's this phone call on here that I want to see if I can get taken off."

I pull up his bill on my computer because I'm nosy like that. Wow. Seventy three minutes. That's quite a little conversation there with a hefty price tag. The outrageousness of our phone prices is something I just can't get behind. Just because we can gouge people does not always mean that we should. (Twelve dollars for a gallon of milk? I'd rather get it straight from the cow.)

"Okay, sir, so you did not make this call?" I have to ask this because it would not be the first time that one of the housekeepers decided to use a guest's phone to catch up with their family. Do

94

they really think that we have no way of finding out, especially with how nosy I am?

"No. I made the call. I just want to see if I can have it taken off the bill."

Sure. While I'm at it, why don't I just comp your whole room because I'm just that nice of a person? "Well, if you made that call, then you have to pay for it. We can't just take the charge off because you asked."

"The thing about it is that I was not made aware that the number and how long the call was would appear on the bill."

"As you can see now, they do."

"Yes, but my wife is going to see this bill and it's very important that she doesn't find out this number."

Ooohhh, I see. It's one of THOSE situations. He doesn't want the wife finding out the little slut's phone number and ruining a perfectly good piece of ass. Someone should have thought about that before having phone sex for seventy three minutes on a hotel phone while they were supposed to be at a work convention. Get a fucking cell phone and don't tell your wife about it. (In the hotel industry you learn a thing or two about gross men cheating.)

"I'm sorry, sir, but you've admitted to making the phone call so there is no way that I can take it off. You are going to have to pay for it."

"What if I tell someone else down there that I didn't make the phone call? Will they be able to take it off for me?"

"Unfortunately, no. They aren't going to believe you because I've already put a comment on your room stating that no one is to take this phone call off your bill." This asshole is really pissing me off. Not only is he trying to weasel out of paying for a phone call to his mistress, but now he's trying to make me an accessory to cheating on his wife. Yeah, that's not going to happen.

"You don't have to do that. I think that is taking it a little…"

"Just hide the bill from your wife. Tell her that our computers crashed and we couldn't print you out a receipt. It happens all the time. Tell her we are going to mail you a copy and pretty soon she will forget about the whole thing." I am, in no way, condoning this man cheating on his wife. He is not attractive enough to be having that much sex. In fact, I'm really hoping that she catches him and takes everything he owns. I'm also thinking about mailing her a copy of the bill with the phone number highlighted. But I won't do that. Bitch, yes. Home wrecker, no.

"If that's all that you can do for me." How full service does he think this hotel is? Fluff your pillow, turn down the bed, cover for your adulterous ass.

Phone. Stop. Fucking. Ringing. I'm sure my voodoo curse is not going to have any effect whatsoever.

"Front desk."

What follows is what I can only assume is some foreign language that I do not have the brain power to understand. I can at least recognize Spanish. I may not understand the language, but I sure know what it is when it is being yelled at me. I can only guess that this is something from the Asian part of the planet.

"I'm sorry, but you're going to have to repeat that and preferably in English because I have no idea what you just said." Polite is officially no longer in my vocabulary.

"I use internet. It free."

This is one of the stupidest things about this hotel. I think we are the only one left in the world that still charges to use the internet. It is not my idea, but from the way people scream at me, you would think I am pocketing all the money from it.

"No. The internet is not free. You have to pay for it."

"But computer say it free."

And who am I to argue with the all-knowing computer. "What computer?"

"When I get room, it say free internet."

I have a sudden flashing realization about what he's saying. There is a package for this hotel that can only be booked through the company website. One of the things it has is free hardwire internet access. The hotel has been trying to get rid of this package for years because they cannot stand giving anything away for free. One quick look at his bill tells me that he, of course, did not use the hardwire internet, but the wireless. "Sir, only the wire internet is free. Not wireless."

"It same thing."

"No it's not. They're different."

"But it free."

97

"No it's not. Only the wire internet is free. Wireless you have to pay for."

"They same thing."

This argument is going nowhere and quickly. There is no way I am going to make him understand and I'm not taking the charge off the bill because I do not feel like being lectured by Doogie. If I wouldn't do it save someone's marriage, why would I do it now?

"They same thing. They same thing. I want free."

"Sir, there is a fundamental difference between hardwire and wireless." Why did I just say that? There is no possible way that he understood any of it. "If you can't see that, then I can't help you." And I hang up the phone.

I'm sure there will a comment card about that one. I have a collection of bad ones about me at home. Turns out I have the tendency to be rather rude to people. Who would have guessed?

If this phone doesn't stop ringing, I am going to rip its cord out of the wall and bring it to the thirtieth floor and throw it off the fucking railing.

"Front desk." My teeth are clenched so hard that I think I might have just chipped a molar.

"I want to see if it's possible to get this movie charge removed from my room."

What the fuck is up with people tonight? Does everyone just think that we are in the habit of giving out free shit all the time because they just don't feel like paying? Is this really how they do things down at the Hilton?

"What was wrong with the movie, sir?"

"I just didn't enjoy it. There weren't any good scenes. I ended up watching the whole thing on fast forward. It just wasn't that great of a movie."

Just say it was porn and get it over with. Like I'm not going to know anyway. Not only can I see the name, but the porno costs like three times more than a regular movie. Besides, you were looking for specific scenes. That's a pretty big clue that you weren't watching Little Miss Sunshine.

"No, sir, I cannot remove the movie." I'm trying to make my voice as dead as possible so that I do not break down into a fit of giggles.

"Why not? I didn't watch it so I should not have to pay for it. That's just not right."

"Did you fast forward through the whole movie? From beginning to end?" Jessie has decided right this second is the appropriate time to listen to my conversation. From what I've just asked, she's figured out what is going on. At least, I assume she has because she is literally shoving her hand in her mouth to stop herself from laughing.

"Yeah. I went straight through it."

"Then congratulations. That means you watched the whole movie. And that means you have to pay for it." I find teasing him in my mock game show voice is the best way of pissing him off as quickly as possible. Jessie finds it amusing too.

"That's bullshit. You can't make me pay for this. I didn't actually watch it."

I raise my voice a little louder than I normally would because I want him to think that someone is going to hear me. "I'm sorry that you didn't enjoy your PORN…excuse me, adult entertainment program, but I just don't see why we have to be responsible because you are pornographically impatient. We are not going to eat that cost. If you would like to dispute this charge again, feel free to speak with the manager when he arrives in the morning, but rest assured that I will explain the situation before you get to him." That's about all that Jessie can take. She quickly runs to the other side of the desk to laugh in the corner. Watching her, it hits me. This is the person whose job it is to make sure I don't speak to the guests like this and she's in the corner laughing her ass off. It's like a well-oiled machine in this place. "Good day, sir."

"But…"

"I said good day." I have always wanted to do that to someone. My inner geek is having a little party.

I hang up the phone and walk away from the desk, ignoring the rest of the lines ringing. I do not have time for this douchebaggery. There's half a pack of cigarettes in my pocket and they sure as shit aren't going to smoke themselves.

Walking to the garage, I realize that I usually storm away from the desk like this at least once a shift. They should probably have a discussion with me about that.

Tonight is not a good night and it was supposed to be because those drug peddlers have finally left. It is one of those shifts where I beg them to let me chain smoke behind the desk, but Doogie says that would be unprofessional. Professionalism doesn't mean a whole lot to me when I have a line of angry guests yelling at me for no reason whatsoever.

"What do you mean room service is closed? What kind of hotel doesn't have twenty-four hour room service?"

"Apparently this kind, ma'am. I cannot change hotel policy. If you would like to complain some more, you are more than welcome to fill out a comment card, and I'll do my best to remember to give it to someone else. But right now, I have a line of people behind you who have real complaints."

Tanya called in sick on me, so I have to play agent and manager. I am in no way enjoying this. Doogie was supposed to stay and help me, but he had some "emergency" with his gorillaesque fiancé. (I've never actually met the woman, but just from talking to her on the phone, I know she's a big chunk of a woman with extensions down to her Baby Got Back ass.) That leaves me alone to deal with the raging bachelorette party for a lesbian couple. This will not end well at all.

Earlier tonight, there was a slight drizzle. Out of fear that those couple of raindrops would turn into a monsoon, they have closed the airport again. What is the point of having an airport if it's closed every time a cloud rolls across the sky? I might be wrong, but I think it is a conspiracy to bug the shit out of me because this is worse than any convention that I have to deal with.

"I want a room with a king sized bed, a minibar, and a hot tub." And I want Lance Bass to walk through the door and carry me away from this pit, but it doesn't look like that's going to happen either.

"I'm sorry, but none of our rooms have minibars or hot tubs. We aren't a resort hotel so we aren't equipped with those things. As for the king bed, I'm afraid we've run out of those for the night."

"What do you mean you've run out? It's bad enough I got shipped here from the airport, but I'm paying good money for this room and I should be able to get whatever I want."

"Ma'am, the price of the room I'm putting you in is three hundred dollars. I think the forty dollar rate that we are giving you is more than generous. We are helping out all the people who were stranded at the airport, so our rooms are first come first serve." I have to explain this every fucking time. It amazes me how people think we have an infinite number of king beds available. Especially when we have two hundred unexpected guests.

"This is the shittiest hotel I've ever had the misfortune of staying in."

"Then, by all means, feel free to stay at the airport. I'm sure the chairs there are just as comfortable as a bed." That idea isn't at all appealing to her. She takes her keys and runs away from me as fast as possible.

The phone has been ringing off the hook for the past half hour. I wish people could master the tricky task of setting an alarm clock. Either that or actually calling the operator for their damn wake up calls. I know it's part of my job to answer the phones, but when I'm trying to do everything in the whole fucking place, it would be nice if I could get a second of peace.

"Excuse me!" A short hobbit of a woman yells out from about halfway through the line. "I've been waiting here for the past twenty minutes."

"And the woman in front of you has been there for twenty five! What's your point?"

Does it not look like I'm working as fast as I can? Do the people in line see more agents behind the desk that I don't? I don't care about professionalism. If this line ever goes down, I am lighting a cigarette. I will hide under the computer if I have to.

It would be one thing if they were complaining about crap that actually mattered, but it is all so stupid. "My room doesn't have a balcony." (None of them do.) "My leftovers from the restaurant are cold." (There's a lovely invention called the microwave. Use it.) "The lobby is filled with cigarette smoke." (Clearly, this is a personal attack against you. I will administer the floggings immediately.)

And then there was Hobbit Woman. She finally waddles her way up the line, so that she can yell at me for something that is in

103

no way my fault. The second she steps in front of me I can smell her breath. It's the rank mixture of whiskey and ass. I can barely breathe without gagging.

"I need to speak to your supervisor."

"Yeah, so do I, but she's decided to spend her time at home with a particularly nasty strand of the imaginary flu, so that means that I'm acting manager on duty."

Her face takes on a certain demon like quality before she lets out this 'weight of the world' sigh. "Well then, you need to do something about that horrible bar manager over there." I'm well aware of who she's talking about seeing as I sexually harass him every night. (Seriously, I am going to be named in a lawsuit.) "He refuses to serve me and my friends." She points her stubby little finger at the flock of lesbians in the bar.

"The bar closes at two. It's ten after now."

"But I still want to drink. I'm a guest in this hotel so I should be able to drink if I want to." I can't take it anymore. Rude or not, I pinch my nose to keep her stank breath from badgering my olfactory senses.

"I understand that, but it's a city law that we aren't allowed to serve alcohol after two a.m."

"I don't give a shit about your city law. I want a fucking drink. And I want you to fire that awful bar manager." Here we go again with the 'I wants'.

"There's two problems here, ma'am. First, we're not all about the illegal stuff here. The two a.m. cutoff time isn't just us being mean. I'd be happy to give you the number to the local police station and they can explain it to you. And second, while it's cute how your thought process is working, I don't have the authority to fire the bar manager."

"Now listen, you little shit." A toxic cloud of her breath surrounds my head. I am seconds away from passing out. "I want him fired right now. This is the most stupidest shit ever. Fuck shit. Shit fuck." I can tell the gallons of alcohol that she's already ingested are really helping her with her argument here.

"Well, I will be sure to tell the hotel manager that it is your whiskey soaked opinion that we let the gentleman go, and I'm sure he'll get right on that."

"I guess that's fucking all I can expect from a fucking fag."

And I was trying to be nice. (Trust me, I was.) Now I have to destroy her and her magic ring too. "Get the fuck out of my face! I do not have time for your stupid ass bullshit! Now go before I slap all the alcohol out of you!"

"Excuse me! But you aren't allowed to talk to me like that. You could lose your job when I talk to the real manager in the morning."

"Yeah, I'm scared. You won't even remember this conversation through your hangover tomorrow. Now don't you have to get back to the Shire, Frodo?"

"Fuck you, you stupid fucking fuck. You are lucky I don't crawl across this desk and beat the shit out of your faggot ass. You will be sorry for the way…"

I can't stop myself. Without realizing I'm doing it, I lean over the desk, not worrying about the stench of her breath. My hand moves faster than her eyes, so she doesn't even know what's happening. I make contact with her sweaty, weird looking face. She falls to the ground from the force of my slap.

I jump up, confused. It's so dark that I can't make anything out, except for the glowing numbers on my clock. Holy shit! Did I really just dream that? This is a very bad sign. Especially seeing as now I have to get up and actually go to work. I hope that this wasn't some kind of eerie premonition because hobbits really creep me out.

I need a fucking vacation.

Sixteen Days of Hate

Dear Mr. Harrison,

I'm writing to take a moment to inform you that your two sons are evil and, at your earliest convenience, you should probably consider having them both destroyed. And if you could make it sooner rather than later, that would give me peace of mind.

While I can tell from the look of you and your family that you are the type of people who usually frequent the Motel 6 variety of hotel, you must remember that this hotel is a little more upscale. I'm glad that you were able to find a room here in your price range on Cheapshit.com or wherever, but there are some things that you really need to change before ever staying here again.

The first thing is that it is not okay to let the kids in your brood run around without shoes or socks. That might fly in the trailer park, but not so much here. I really have no desire to see your ingrown toenail. Also, I understand that this is Texas and all, but I don't think the cowboy hat is actually necessary. I'm pretty sure everyone knows you're a hick.

Now as to why I think your sons need to be put to sleep. Please hear me out before trying to defend the little monsters. I'm well aware of how cool going somewhere like a hotel can be. I was a kid once myself. But by the teenage years, as your kids are obviously in, they should at least have some idea of how to act in a public place. I assume you have taken them to Wal-Mart before. Proper behavior in a hotel like this does not include throwing things off the twenty sixth floor to see if they break. And I do understand that the lighter that they threw was an anniversary present from your wife, but you are still not going to get it back. You should have thought about that before you gave it to your son. It is now the property of The Hotel.

It is also in no way acceptable for your demon spawn to have thrown a hunk of chocolate cake over the railing. While it is not very likely that the cake will cause any damage that does not comfort me when it hits me in the head. And it doesn't help when they deny doing it, like I wouldn't be able to tell who was throwing things at me in a completely empty lobby. If they didn't want to get caught, then perhaps they shouldn't have hung over the railing to laugh as it rained chocolate.

It is for these reasons that I firmly believe you should put both of the boys to sleep. I'm sure there is a pound or something that will do it for you. I think this is the best solution for you, me, and the rest of the world. While you are at it, you may want to consider having yourself sterilized so that we don't have this problem again in the future.

Thanks in advance

Sean

P.S. It is for these reasons and these reasons alone that you were asked to leave the hotel, not because I am a "fucking cocksucking butt pirate." It is simply because you and your ill-conceived children are hicks.

They won't give me a vacation because I haven't worked here long enough. What has only been four months feels like decades of my life that I will never get back. After that nightmare I had a couple weeks ago, they have become more and more frequent. Each night is a dive into my psyche, giving me picture of what I really want to do while at work, from lighting up a cigarette behind the front desk to throwing things at Lily in Room Service. It is only a matter of time before I actually start doing some of these things.

While they won't give me the full vacation to some tropical beach resort that I so deserve, I was able to talk them into giving me four days off in a row. It was simply a matter of sitting down with Doogie and explaining that "if I don't get some kind of break from this place, I will hurt somebody. I'm not saying that it will be you, but the chances of that are very high." (And I wonder why he always hated me.) Needless to say, the next schedule came out with me being off from Wednesday through Sunday. It's amazing how a really well placed threat can get you what you want.

What makes this so much better is that this week is Thanksgiving. And I will be off for it. Not that I have any big holiday plans, except for lounging around in sweatpants and watching Veronica Mars on DVD. (I love her. She's got spunk.) The idea is to spend zero amount of time thinking about The Hotel and hotel related incidents, with the exception of throwing darts at the picture of Doogie I have on my wall. (I don't really have one, but doesn't it sound cool, like I'm an often thwarted super villain or something. No?)

But as with most things that are good in this world, my dreams are dashed by Doogie. "Sean, we've had a little bit of a situation here today and we were hoping that you would be able to come in tonight. It would really help us out."

He, of course, calls me at two o'clock in the afternoon. Something that he has yet to realize is that the afternoon is the middle of the night for me. Him calling me at this time is like me calling him at three in the morning. (Which I have done. It turns out that his fiancé doesn't particularly care for him receiving late night text messages asking, "What you wearing, Daddy?") Though he might have realized this and did it on purpose because he knew I would be half asleep and agree to anything just to shut him up. Yeah, I'm really that stupid.

"What kind of situation?" Because I am that kind of nosy. (We've discussed this, no?)

"I can't really get into it right now. Some things happened today that I'm not allowed to talk about."

"If I'm about to give up one of my days off, I think I have a right to know why. Especially seeing as how hard those days were to pry away from you." Many people ask me why I antagonize Doogie the way I do. The answer is, of course, because it is a hell of a lot of fun.

"Please, Sean."

111

Oh damn. Things must be really bad because Doogie has never once said "Please" to me. (Or "thank you", for that matter. He's quite rude.) Maybe that's why I tell him yes, I'm so shocked by his sudden manners. Either that or the larger number on my paycheck.

"But I reserve the right to bitch and moan about it."

And I do. I can't get back to sleep because something in Doogie's voice sets off a chemical reaction in my brain that won't allow me a moment's peace. So I bitch about that too, calling anyone who will listen. And when I realize that no one cares, I write something bitchy about Doogie to post on my blog. After that, I just sort of bitch to myself because no one will listen. (Veronica Mars feels my pain.)

When I grow tired of bitching, I decide it's time to figure out what the big shit is that happened. The only thing I can think of is that there has been some form of bloodshed. Since they were left with no other choice but to give me the days off, even though the guy who takes my place is out of town, the only option was to put the two managers on the shift together. The thing that makes this so good is that Jessie and Tanya cannot stand each other. I was thinking about coming to work anyway just to see the blows between them. So I assumed that something happened between them before they even had to work together. And if they thought I wasn't going to be in the middle of it, then they would be wrong.

On the way to work, I'm driving down the interstate, hating all the people who are on the road at ten o'clock on a Wednesday night and jamming to my iPod. (Nothing gets me in the mood to go to work like a playlist that includes Kelly Clarkson, Reba McEntire, Olivia Newton John, and the collected works of School House Rock. Yes, people stare.) I'm trying to sing out some of my frustrations so I'm not a complete ass clapper at work.

When I get there, I'm not even allowed behind the front desk. Instead, Doogie manhandles me with his curiously small hands and drags me into the back office. The way I'm sitting in the chair with him standing over me makes me feel like I'm in some fucked up Law and Order episode.

"Thank you for coming in tonight. We appreciate your help. This is what's going on. Tanya is being fired right now."

That I didn't see coming. Sure, she probably needed to go. Her attitude makes mine seem downright pleasant. She's always disappearing, so I'm basically doing her job most of the time. She's always late and trying to leave early. Since they didn't try to fire her before, I just assumed they didn't care. But apparently, checking herself into a suite (Not a room. A suite.) for a couple weeks is more than they are willing to put up with.

The sad thing about this is the only reason she got caught is because she put the suite in her own name. If she would have just put a fake name down, no one would have known a thing. The managers usually don't pay attention to the rooms that are given out for free, which explains how she got away with it for two weeks.

At least I won't have to have any more racially charged debates about Flavor of Love.

"So thank you again. We appreciate the sacrifice that you are making because you won't be getting a day off this week."

Hold up. I agreed to come to work tonight. Where's he getting this bullshit that I'm giving up all my days off? That was not part of our arrangement. The sneaky little bastard tricked me. It is so on now.

I calm myself by thinking about the paycheck. That will be at least two whole shifts that are completely overtime. I could do it for the money. And really, how hard could it be?

Famous last words.

**

Since I've already worked for five days I'm calling this
Day Six

I really wish this bitch would stop coughing in my face. It's not that I'm not thoroughly enjoying this rousing conversation about her boyfriend back home in Montana who she thinks is cheating on her (He so is.), but I'm not really looking to catch whatever communicable disease she's throwing out into the world. My lungs get enough punishment from chain smoking, thank you very much.

While trying to tune this woman's inane ramblings out, I've decided to plan as many horrible deaths for Doogie as I can possibly come up with. There's one plan that I really want to try, but I have no idea how to get my hands on five hundred electric eels. It's a shame because it is a really good plan. It involves…

"Hey, I need a new key. Mine don't work no more." I'm willing to look past the double negative if it means that I can get rid of this guy faster. Because, between the two of them, I'd rather listen to 'My man is cheating on me with a snowman' girl. (What is there in Montana?)

I look up his room number and, right away, I see something is wrong. But it takes me a little bit to actually realize what it is. And then, it slaps me right in the face. There is no way in hell that this man's name is Fred Flintstone.

I should probably mention that, every once in a while, we get famous people who stay with us. When they come to stay, we are given meeting after meeting about how we are to respect their privacy, not make a big deal about their presence, and never, under penalty of death, ask for their autograph. (I was firm on my stance that all bets were off should I ever come face to face with Lance Bass.) And a lot of these people use aliases to cement the fact that they are just like everyone else.

This is a concept that I'm okay with. Seeing as how the hotel overcharges them because they can, the least I can do is let them use a fake name. (I always planned on using the alias Bitchy McShutTheFuckUp.) The problem I'm having with this is that I have no idea who this person is, so I can't figure out why he would need an alias.

Instead of arguing and asking for an I.D. that is clearly not going to say Fred Flintstone, I just give him a key and send him on his way. (There is seriously going to be an entire Dateline devoted to me.) But now the real quest begins. Because I'm nosy, I want to know who the fuck he is and why I'm supposed to care about him.

After a great deal of exhaustive research (basically walking ten feet and asking Jessie), it turns out that this guy was on a television show whose name no one can remember. Apparently it was so bad that they just cancelled it right in the middle of the broadcast. They just went to commercial break and never came back. (Not really, but wouldn't that be funny.)

So this guy was on a show that no one cared about. Now he's in a play downtown that no one is going to see. According to Jessie, he's been trying to give away tickets to everyone in the hotel and no one wants them. The only reason Jessie knows him is because the managers had a meeting about it. Why exactly does he need an alias? Certainly not because paparazzi are trying to break down the doors.

I've decided to file this away as one of those things in life that I can neither explain nor put forth the effort to try.

***

Day Seven

It's Thanksgiving Day and my dreams of spending the whole day with Veronica Mars is in the past. Instead I am being forced to spend it with people who are grumpy because they have to spend their holiday in a hotel. (Unless I'm the one doing the bitching, I don't want to hear it.)

"Excuse me, but I was under the impression that this hotel does not allow pets." This woman is talking in one of those snooty voices that you think only exists on The Simpsons. This does not make me more inclined to help her. In fact, it kind of makes me hate her a little more.

"Yes, ma'am, you're correct. We do not allow pets here."

"Then can you explain to me why there is a dog barking in the room next door to mine?"

Could it be that there is a dog in the room? Does she think that we pump the sound of barking in some rooms just for ambiance? "I don't know, ma'am, but I will investigate immediately and have the dog removed."

"See that you do!"

Bitch.

Instead of doing something I could easily do myself, I make Jessie do it. I just can't be troubled. And seeing as how I'm not even supposed to be here today, they are going to kiss my ass just for showing up.

Here's what I love about Jessie. When she comes back downstairs to tell me that, lo and behold, she can hear a dog barking from inside the room (The woman may have been a snob, but I didn't think she was making it up.), she doesn't bother asking questions. She just changes the lock on the door. This is genius and just the right amount of bitchy. I'm dying to see the blowout that ensues because of this.

And I must be doing something right because I don't have to wait long at all. I barely have time to really work out the details of a Doogie destruction plan that involves a sledgehammer and a hot iron before someone comes up to the desk complaining that they can't get into their room. And if it isn't Mr. Flintstone. What have I done to get rewarded with so much joy? Whatever it is, I am doing it every day from now on.

"Yeah. My key isn't working again. This is the second time in two days. What is the matter with the keys?" Dammit. Why don't I ever think to bring popcorn to work?

"Well, sir, tonight I had to change the locks to ensure that you came down here to speak with me." Jessie is attempting to do the whole polite thing, but I can tell that right beneath the surface there is a thick layer of hate. "This is in regards to the fact that there is a small dog in your room."

"So? What about it?"

"Pets are not allowed in this hotel."

"Well, none of you bitches told me that."

118

Is it my birthday and no one told me? This is like the best day ever. The sight of Jessie's face morphing from polite to destroy is like the greatest thing in the world. "Yes, they did tell you. Our sales person told your group leader on several occasions that pets weren't allowed here because you kept asking to bring your dog. If you would like a reminder of that I do have copies of the e-mails that were sent."

"Don't you feel like an ass!" That was so not supposed to come out of my mouth. Mr. Flintstone does not seem to have found it amusing in the least.

"Shut up, fag." This, right here, is the moment that, were I a woman, the earrings would be coming off. It is so beyond on. "That doesn't give you the right to go in my room."

Jessie opens her mouth to respond, but I beat her to it. This asshat is about to get a one way ticket to Bedrock with a foot up his ass. "No one went in your room. We've been getting complaints all night." (It's only a small lie.)

"How is it that you knew it was a small dog if you didn't go inside to see it?"

"Because you can tell the difference between a big dog and a small dog barking." Did I really just have to explain that to another human being?

"So are you some kind of dog expert?"

"No, but I'm not a fucking moron." Jessie doesn't even care what I say to him anymore. Her opinion is as long as the first swear comes out of the guest's mouth, I can say whatever the hell I want. In fact, she's backing off to let me handle this myself.

"Do you have any idea who I am?"

"No, I don't. And I can't find anyone who can tell me. And even if I did know who you are, it wouldn't change the fact that you have five minutes to get the dog out of your room or you will be forced to leave. And, on top of that, you will be charged two hundred dollars for a deep cleaning fee because you brought an animal into your room."

"You can't charge me extra."

"The hell I can't. If you had bothered to read the signs in your room, you would see that it tells you about the pet fee."

He bangs his fist against the front desk. Yeah, like that is going to help his case any. "I am never staying in another one of these hotels again. You just lost yourself a big client. Big client!"

"But where will you stay when you do your extensive work as an extra on Lifetime Original Movies." Does he think I am going to try and beg him to stay? I'm hoping that I never have to see this douche bag again. (Goodness knows I'm not going to turn on the TV and find him there.)

"First thing in the morning, I am filing a complaint with your boss. I don't care what the rules are. You do not have a right to invade my privacy by going into my room and messing with my dog. And I will not be paying extra charges you put on my bill. So don't expect to have a job tomorrow."

Now he's got me shaking in my shoes. Does he really think I'm scared of a guy who played Brandy's boyfriend in one episode of Moesha? I think not. "You do that. You file your little complaint. But don't be surprised when they laugh in your face for flat out admitting you broke the rules that were spelled out for you multiple times. And they will be able to print a report of how many times your lock was opened so you can see for yourself that no one went into your room. Now get out of my face."

I don't know why he actually listens to me this time, but I'm glad to see him storm away from the front desk. I'm not going to lie. That was fun. If I could have a fight like that every night, I may never have to have another cigarette again. Doogie is so not going to approve. (File that under: Shit, don't give a.)

I put on the most pompous face I can muster and leave it there for the ten minutes that it takes him to get his creepy, Taco Bell dog out of the hotel. (Don't think I didn't notice that he took longer than I told him he had.) After he hands off the dog to one of his friends, he sits in the bar, leaving the seat next to him empty for his ego.

This presents an interesting situation. Since I have finished my paperwork and have nothing left to do, I am free to stand here and stare at him. And what's he going to do about it. He can't complain because someone is looking at him. (Okay, technically, he can. But only if he wants to be a big, fat baby.)

Jessie comes back behind the front desk. Because I wasn't paying attention (and trying to shoot death rays at Mr. Flintstone

121

with my eyes), I didn't notice that she's been walking around doing managery things. "You know he's talking about you over there. He said something about the evil fag at the front desk and how he is going to make sure you get fired. He said that when he's finished you will be lucky to get a job at McDonald's."

"I'll remember that while he's doing Shakespeare in the Parking Garage."

***

Day Eight

Walking in the office, I can automatically tell something is not right. Where there are usually just the sounds of people's souls being sucked away, there are now people laughing. The back office is not really a place that exudes happiness. It's more the perfect place for a joyless death. But I don't remember falling into an alternate reality, so someone must really be laughing.

It's two people actually. Grace and Doogie look like they are about to fall out of their chairs. Doogie's face does not look natural. I don't think I've ever seen him smile, much less laugh. I feel like I'm in the presence of evil.

They see me standing here and start laughing harder. Grace has to grab her side and has a pained look on her face. I've had nightmares in elementary school that started off this exact same way. It doesn't really comfort me to know that it is coming true in

122

my adult life. All I need to make this complete is some pointing and someone to try and give me a wedgie.

"What the hell is so funny?"

Instead of saying anything, which would require them to stop laughing, Grace hands me a sheet of paper. It's a printed out e-mail.

To: Front_Desk_Manager@thehotel.com
From: Not_Denzel_Washington@bigbaby.com

I am very disturbed by some of the behavior that I have witnessed tonight. I was never informed that your hotel does not allow pets, so I brought my dog, Sprinkles, to stay with me. Tonight I was maliciously locked out of my room by your horrible front desk person. Then he rudely told me that I had to remove my dog from the hotel.

When I returned to my room, I found Sprinkles in a very agitated state. He denies it, but I know the guy at the front desk came into my room and messed with my dog. I also suspect there has been some molestation of a sexual nature. I do not find this to be appropriate behavior of a hotel.

Due to the trauma that Sprinkles has sustained in your hotel, she will need extensive therapy. I don't know if I will ever be able to stay in your hotel ever again after everything that I have suffered here. And I know that it would be a great loss for you to lose valuable business like mine, but I'm afraid that is how it must be.

I would consider it a personal favor if you ensure that the despicable guy who worked the front desk tonight no longer has a job.

Thank you
Fred Flintstone

I am conflicted. I don't know if I should start laughing or be really pissed off. This guy really has some nerve calling me a fag when he's the one who has a dog named Sprinkles that he's about to put into therapy. That part is kind of funny, but I don't particularly enjoy being accused of dog molestation.

After careful consideration of all the facts involved, I have decided the correct course of action is to become thoroughly pissed off. This isn't the best time because I still haven't finalized my plans for Doogie's destruction and they will suffer if I have to split my focus. Maybe I could kidnap his dog or something. That wouldn't require too much effort on my part, then Doogie's demise could stay at the forefront of my mind. I must keep my priorities straight.

"I'm hoping that we don't actually need to have a meeting about this." It might just be my imagination, but I think Grace may have snorted into her hand.

"You know me. I've never met a dog I could resist."

There are many things that are unknown in this world. Is there life on other planets? Who built Stonehenge? Why is Britney Spears insane? But there is one thing that is certain. Mr. Flintstone is so getting a three a.m. wake up call.

***

Day Eight 3:04 A.M.

"Good morning, Front Desk. This is Sean. How may I assist you?" I lay on the nice extra thick because I can see it is Mr. Flintstone calling.

"Do you have any idea what time it is?"

"Yes, sir. It's 3:04 in the morning. Is there anything else I can assist you with?"

"Why did I just get a call in my room saying that it was my three a.m. wake up call?"

"In the computer, it shows that you requested a wake up call for this time." This is in no way true, but I've been

125

working on making myself sound convincing ever since I put the wake up call in the system a couple of hours ago. Which just proves that I am a better actor then he is.

"I most certainly did not. Why would I request a wake up call when I only got to sleep an hour ago? This is ridiculous."

"Well, I don't know what to tell you, sir. Maybe your dog did it. You know how they tend to act up after they've experienced sexual trauma."

Immediately, I hear the sharp inhale of breath over the phone that tells me he has no business calling anyone a fag. Only gay men do the gay inhale. "It was you who put the wake up call in. I know it was."

"Prove it." I slam the phone down before I start laughing.

This is the reason why I've decided that it is okay to blatantly taunt this man. Of all the things that I actually did that he has a right to complain about, he chose to make up a stupid ass accusation. Like anyone is going to believe that I would jeopardize my job so that I could "get with" his dog. Now who is going to believe a word that comes out of his mouth?

I win.

***

Day Nine

Fred Flintstone has checked out and I am just devastated. He got an emergency call from his agent and he needed to rush off right away to play Man on Bus #2 on an episode of Smallville. It's not really that big of a loss because no one was going to see his stupid play anyway. The understudy is probably twice as good as his dumb ass.

But with the loss of Mr. Flintstone, we have gained an even greater evil. This is something that strikes fear in the very bottom of my heart. Children. Lots and lots of children.

They are everywhere. Running around the lobby. Throwing things off the railings. Screaming bloody murder just to hear the echo. I haven't even clocked in yet and I've already been hit in the head with a bunch of crumpled up phone book pages. I can see it now. Tonight is going to be the night that I'm going to go to jail for hurting one of the guests.

I've locked myself in the office for a few minutes to get away from the swarm. (I think they can smell fear.) I should be at the front desk, but since I'm not getting paid to be here at the moment, screw it. I never signed on to deal with a flock of children. It's the same as with the hooker thing. There are some things that weren't in the job description.

127

Preparing myself the best that I can, I go back outside. Immediately, I am attacked by a group of girls who have fashioned themselves after the Bratz dolls, except with no shoes. (Gross.) They want to know where the pool is and the second I tell them it's closed, they turn on me. With the levels of hate they are shooting at me, you would swear I just told them that Justin Timberlake is gay. What hotel is going to let you swim in the middle of the night anyway?

After getting the lowdown from Jessie, I find out that all these kids are here with the same group. The SMILE Youth Ministries is having their retreat here this year. This means for the next couple of days we will be infested with these little monsters. I get the feeling that this is going to be very detrimental to my attitude.

"Um, excuse me." This blond girl is standing at the desk, but I can't focus on her because her high pitched, valley girl voice is drilling into my skull. "We were wondering if there was any place around here where we could do some cheerleading practice."

"Um…no." Even if there was, why would we allow cheerleading practice to take place after midnight? Because we've got spirit? No, we don't.

"But you don't understand. Mindy just broke up with Conner and she's been really off for the past two weeks. Coach said that if she doesn't get better soon, she's going to be replaced with Shelly Brinkmeyer. And Coach just can't do that. Mindy is totally my BFF and Shelly is so stupid. We have to practice all we can."

OMG! Can you imagine the horror of having to do cheerleading without your BFF? And how dare that stupid Shelly think she can take Mindy's place? It is problems like this that put the whole war thing in perspective. Obviously we have issues at home that we should be dealing with first.

"There's no room big enough for that open right now. Maybe during the day something can be worked out, but not right now."

"This place sucks. Why are we even staying here?"

Apparently because the powers that be hate me. I can think of no other explanation as to why I am being subjected to children. That is the beauty of being gay. Children are not part of the equation. Don't get me wrong, kids are okay. I've been known to play with some now and again. I can love a child as long as I can give it back when its cuteness grows tiresome. I don't want to have to feel guilty for wanting to pass my own kid on to someone more responsible than me. And let's face it, it's not like I could carry it around in a bag on my shoulder. It's not a dog and I'm not Paris Hilton.

What's really amazing to me is how all of these girls have the exact same voice. They all have the high pitched, squeaky voice that makes me want to rip my ears off. Either that or poke myself in the forehead over and over

129

again until I finally break through my skull and stick my finger in my brain. Either way would be less painful than hearing approximately a hundred girls doing the exact same valley girl laugh at the exact same time. It's like hell in surround sound.

Hours and hours of listening to them talking and laughing are giving me a headache. A cigarette won't even help me now. The only thing that would make any difference is if I could somehow do my job while wearing a blindfold and ear plugs. But I'm sure Doogie would find that very unprofessional. (And he can totally suck it.)

"We want to watch a movie." I am staring directly at what looks to be a twelve year old girl who decided to take her fashion advice from Britney Spears. (Basically, a twelve year old hooch.) "We want to watch *The Devil Wears Prada*, but the TV says we have to talk to you to get our movies unlocked. So unlock them." This is the number one reason that I am not having children. It is taking everything in my power not to call this little girl a bitch. Because that would be wrong. But Little Miss Attitude better watch herself.

"The rooms are already paid for by your sponsors, but to unlock the movies and phones, you have to leave a form of payment."

"We'll pay for it when we leave."

"It doesn't work like that. You have to leave payment up front to guarantee that it gets paid for."

She really thinks staring me down is going to accomplish her goal. She seems to have forgotten that I'm taller than her, bigger than her, and not afraid to sit on her. We'll see who has the attitude then.

"Here." She throws a crumpled up five dollar bill on the front desk.

"Five dollars isn't going to cover it. We require a minimum cash deposit of fifty dollars or a credit card to be left on file." We only require a thirty dollar deposit, but I don't feel like making life easy for this girl.

"But I only have five dollars."

"Then how exactly did you plan on paying for the movie?"

"We were going to ask our chaperone for the money, if you must know."

"Then go get the money now."

"This is such bullshit."

I can't lie, I'm a little shocked. My mouth hangs open. And then I find my words. "OH! Aren't you here with a church, little girl? Does God know you have such a little potty mouth? I'll tell you one thing. You are going to go straight to hell. And when you do, I will be the one throwing rocks at you for all eternity. Now go wash your mouth out with soap."

The little girl looks at me like I just slapped her across the face. "Um, you can't talk to me like that. Isn't it your job to be nice to me?"

"Do you really want to get a head start on me throwing rocks at you?"

"I'm telling my chaperone what you just said to me."

"God doesn't like little girls who tattle either."

The little potty mouth runs off back to the elevators. I'd feel bad about yelling at her, but I already know I'm going to hell, so I might as well try to get the best seats I can manage.

It's really true what they say. Children are a sexually transmitted disease.

***

Day Thirteen

I remember going on field trips when I was a kid. Granted, they were dorky field trips that involved academic challenges (NERD!), but they were still trips. We even stayed in nice hotels like this one. I do not, however, recall being allowed to act a total ass while on these school sponsored outings.

Obviously things have changed quite a bit since I was a kid. (Why do I suddenly feel the need to crochet an afghan and use the phrase whipper snappers?)

There is an entire herd of children stampeding around the hotel. I can hear the pounding of their feet as they run around the third floor. They are slowly working their way up the entire hotel. This is highly annoying because the last time I checked I didn't work in a grazing meadow. The only solution I see is to shoot them all with tranquilizer darts. Possibly even brand a couple of them.

Jessie has been given the night off, which sort of makes me very angry because if anyone should be able to stay in bed, it's me. Grace has been given the honor of taking over the night shift while Jessie sleeps for two reasons. One: she has the least seniority of all the managers. And two: everyone knows how pissed off I am, and they think I won't yell at someone who is as nice as she is. Damn them for being right. Grace is far too sweet and soft spoken for me to vent my anger at her. This is bad because the only people left for me to take it out on are the kids.

The phone has been ringing nonstop since I've gotten here with people complaining about the kids making noise. "Why can't you keep these kids quiet? Aren't you in charge around here? I'm trying to get some rest here and it's impossible. I expect something to be done immediately."

I'm too tired to argue with this lady. Besides she has a valid point. These kids should be under some sort of curfew. I would like to know why the chaperones are not watching them. Isn't that their only purpose on this trip?

We have the overnight security guard roaming the floors trying to corral the little monsters. But he is two seconds from useless. And he also thinks that twenty dollars an hour is not enough money for him to do any actual work. That leaves it up to my nine dollar and fifty cent an hour ass to do his job. (Grace is far too nice to yell at children. Me, not so much.)

Now I have to patrol the halls like some underappreciated hall monitor. I'm not too pleased about this turn of events, and it must really show on my face because the very few adults that I've passed have looked scared of me. The kids, however, do not seem to be burdened by fear.

The elevator doors open on the twenty-fourth floor and all I see is a blur of four boys running down the hall.

"HEY!" I scream so loudly that one of them trips over his own feet. I have to fight so I don't laugh and completely ruin this mask of righteous anger that I have going on. "What do you think you're doing? This is not your house. You can't just run around screaming and hollering. Where's your chaperone?"

The four boys line up in front of me with their heads hanging. They look like perfect angels. It seems that they are truly sorry for what they have done and learned a valuable lesson. Clearly, this is bullshit and a rather obvious ruse to make me let them go without getting into trouble. They have forgotten that I hate them and everything they stand for, so that tired little routine will not work on me. "He's in the room."

"Then let's go."

We all climb back in the elevator and travel to the fifteenth floor. The second the doors open the kids take off running. It's a good thing that I'm not as stupid as they would like to think I am. I have my hand ready to grab the closest one by his collar before he can get too far. He also happens to be the smallest so he makes the perfect hostage.

Because his friends can't leave him behind, they reluctantly walk back over to us. This shows that, in some small way, these kids are better than me because I would have ditched my friend so fast. It's good to know that they at least have some morals. Though I'm pretty sure that Small Fry is the rich one of the group and his friends know that if they ditch him, he won't buy them stuff anymore.

"Don't try that again. Take me to your room."

I follow them to the very last room on the hallway and wait for them to open the door. The whole time I have a firm grip on Small Fry so none of them can get away.

135

When they get inside, I see that the lights are, of course, off. "Mr. Eric is asleep."

"Then wake him up."

I let go of Small Fry and he runs in the room. They try to close the door on me. Like I'm going to fall for that one. I quickly stick my foot in to keep the door open. Because of the way the room is shaped I cannot see where the beds are, but I don't hear any movement whatsoever. These kids honestly think that I'm as stupid as they are.

The lead monster comes back to the door. "He won't wake up. I think he took some sleeping pills." It seems that they are also incapable of learning.

I lean over and put my face as close to his as I can get it. "Get in there and wake him up or I will do it myself. And trust me, he will be a lot angrier if I wake him up the way I want to."

Finally the boy has learned fear. This time it only takes a minute for them to get Mr. Eric out of bed. And it only takes me a couple seconds to come to the conclusion that Mr. Eric is a douche.

"What's this about?"

"Can you explain why these four boys were found running around the twenty-fourth floor while you are in bed?' Right now, any obligation that I have to be nice to this person means nothing.

"They were here when I went to bed. I can't watch them all the time."

"See, that's where you are wrong. You can. You are their chaperone. It is your job to watch them all the time."

"I have to sleep. They can stay awake longer than me." I see that Mr. Eric is about as smart as the kids he is supposed to be watching.

"Then you should have thought about that before you signed up for this. I'm sure the organizers of this event will be very happy to hear about how you were allowing the kids to run around without supervision."

"It's not that big of a deal. So what if the kids were running around. They weren't bothering anyone." Mr. Eric clearly thinks that he is going back to bed soon so he wants to get rid of me as quickly as possible.

"Yes, they were. In fact, they were bothering an entire floor of people. I don't think that those people are paying for the honor of listening to these boys running around acting like asses." I sound dangerously close to caring about the other guests. This is just another reason to hate these kids.

"They're kids. What am I going to do?"

"Your job. You are an adult, aren't you?" I use the word adult very loosely because it looks like Mr. Eric went through puberty yesterday. "So I would make sure that these boys don't leave this room again tonight. If that

137

means that you have to do without a little sleep, deal with it. I'm warning you now. If I see one of these kids running around the hotel again, you will be kicked out immediately. Then they can run around the street corner with the prostitutes." In no way do I have the authority to kick them out, but it makes for such a nice threat. And he doesn't know that I have absolutely no power. He can just assume I'm the manager because I'm wearing a butt ugly tie.

I storm off. As much as I would like to scream at Mr. Eric and his posse of evil some more, there are other kids needing to be yelled at.

On my way to the twelfth floor to break up a group who have decided to play a game of 'Who Wants To Be Annoying?' I pass by this girl and boy sitting outside of a room. Unable to break from tradition the girl is dressed like a complete whore. From the way she is sitting, I can see glitter outlined words on her ass. (Words on the ass are the devil. All the things wrong with the world that cannot be blamed on Meredith Grey can be blamed on words on the ass.) The boy's hands are moving into places that these preteens shouldn't even know exist.

"Get in your room before I call your chaperone out here." I would stay and give them a thorough bitching out, but those kids on twelve are getting louder. "Nasty." That last part was supposed to be part of an inner monologue, but it didn't really work out like that.

Since it is only a couple flights down, I take the stairs. This way I can surprise the kids and possibly even scare the shit out of them at the same time. Though this doesn't work out like I planned either. They have apparently set up a lookout because the second I walk around the corner, they bolt. This tells me that these little shits know they are doing something wrong and they chose to do it anyway. For this, they must die.

I chase after them. (Just a note: Do not make a fat man run after you. This will not make him happy.) They are pretty confident in the fact that I am never going to catch them. And yes, they might be smaller and faster than me, but I am smarter than them by a lot. All I have to do is run to the other side of the hotel. There I can look over the railing and see what is happening on every floor. That would include the seventeen prepubescent donkeys trying to duck and run one floor down. Like I would never see all of them trying to squeeze through the door at the same time.

By the time I get to the room, they have managed to cram everyone inside and slam the door. Why do they assume that everyone in the world is as stupid as they are? I roll my eyes and knock. "Hotel manager." At this point, I might as well go for broke with the lying.

"Shhhh! Be quiet. He won't know we're in here."
Because there is no way that I would ever hear that. What
do they think this door is made out of anyway?

"You might as well open the door. I have a key."
(Master keys are awesome!)

They don't listen. This is really not the best night to
assume that I'm bluffing. I stick the key in and open the
door. Just like I thought, they are too dumb to have put the
chain on so I can get right in. And, in unison, seventeen
kids shit on themselves.

"OUT!"

They know that they are busted and that I am pissed.
Outside in the hall, I make them sit in a line against the
wall by the elevators. One by one, they call their
chaperones to come pick them up. While we wait, I pace in
front of them with a murderous look on my face. I would
make such a good ruthless dictator.

I'm not surprised at all when the chaperones come and
the kids get in absolutely no trouble. All of them, including
the adults, get the same yelling at as that douche bag, Mr.
Eric. They don't care one bit, but it still feels good to yell at
them. Righteous anger and all that.

I decide to do one last patrol before I give up for the
night. This hotel does not pay me nearly enough to deal
with this level of bullshit. I barely get paid enough to show
up.

Maybe word has traveled that there is some mean ass fat guy walking around and yelling at people because the noise has quieted down a bit. There is still some noise, but not enough for me to actually care about. I'm not going to strain my voice unless it is really worth it.

And then I see them. Little Miss Glittery Words on Her Ass with her boyfriend lying on top of her making out in the hallway. And I'm not talking about little kisses. They are full on trying to swallow each other whole. You usually don't see this high concentration of gross outside of porn. Don't kids come equipped with chastity belts to keep this kind of shit from happening?

They are so into what they are doing that they don't notice me walk up to them or when I squat down to where my head is right next to theirs. They do notice when I clear my throat. There is something about the sight of kids shitting on themselves that makes me smile.

"Perhaps you didn't hear me before or maybe you just don't grasp the English language that well, but I'm going to give you one last chance. You have exactly five seconds to get in your room or I will drag your big, shiny ass down to the lobby where we will contact every living relative you have so you can explain what you were doing here."

Her boyfriend ditches her. (And who said chivalry was dead?) He runs down the hall so fast you would think I have a gun or something. But I don't care about him. I have the girl cornered. She's having trouble getting the key in the door because her hand is shaking so badly. I'm right behind her, not giving her an inch of freedom. She finally gets the door open, runs inside, and slams it in my face.

It might have been sexist of me to go after the girl that way, but I don't think so. Sure, the boy was just as guilty of whoriness as she was, but there was one very big difference between them. He did not have words on his ass; therefore he didn't offend me nearly as much.

It has been such a stressful night that I'm going to do something that I've never done before. I pull out a cigarette and light it right here in the hall. I don't care that it is against the rules. I don't care if this is a nonsmoking floor. I don't care if Doogie walks around the corner and catches me right now. The only thing that matters is that for right now I am in a place where there are no kids. That's nice.

***

Day Fourteen

It's quiet. Never before has silence been so wonderful. I don't know how the chaperones got them to obey a curfew tonight, nor do I care. I'm sure they used tales of the horrible creature who roams the halls at night yelling at bad children. So be it. It just gets me closer to my goal of all children fearing me.

I pull up a chair at the front desk and relax. I even brought my iPod inside, just in case I needed to calm myself down. Luckily all I need it for is to have something to listen to while I write mean things about the kids for my blog.

Grace and I have decided that we are going to have a quiet night if it kills us. It seems that last night while I was upstairs yelling at children, Grace was at the front desk getting screamed at by everyone else in the hotel for letting the kids run around. Because I can see how it's our fault that they were raised to be assholes.

"Sean, can you pull the check-in cards for all the people you checked in tonight? I can't find one of the guests in the computer and I need to get some credit card information."

"Mr. Crotchfelt is in room 1622."

"How in the world did you remember that off the top of your head?"

"He's the only person that I checked in tonight. And a name like Crotchfelt tends to be remembered."

It takes Grace a couple of seconds to understand what I'm saying. She finally gets the joke and starts to giggle. Poor Grace. She's so sweet that she always misses great opportunities to make fun of people. (But how do you pass up Crotchfelt?)

A strange noise starts echoing through the lobby. It sounds like music, but I'm not sure it would really be welcome in the music family. This is the kind of strange sound that you would hear if life were a fairy tale and evil was being plotted against you. And unless, I'm the wicked witch, this is no fairy tale.

Without even looking at Grace, I leave to go find where the noise is coming from. The beauty of having glass elevators is that I don't have to do a whole lot of searching. I can just ride up and down until I see who is making the offending noise. (It's like a search party for the lazy.) The downside is that there is only a sheet of glass between me and a certain death.

On the twenty-third floor, I can see two people sitting in the hall with what looks like a guitar. The noise is louder here, so I know that this is where it's coming from. I go around the back way so they don't have a chance to run away when they see me. The element of surprise is my friend.

As I get closer, I can hear that the guy is singing. (And very poorly at that.) What told him this was the appropriate time and place to practice?

"What are you doing?" My voice takes on an unnatural sound. It is a little too Ursula the Sea Witch for my taste. "You do realize this is a hotel, don't you?"

The doofus jumps back and drops his guitar. Just from first impression alone, I can tell that neither his looks nor his voice are going to get this teenager laid anytime soon. And the girl he's with is totally butt ug, so that's really the best that he can hope for.

"What's the problem, big man? I was just working on a song."

A word to the wise. When you are dealing with a pissed off fat guy, the way to calm him down is not to call him 'big man'. It is not cute. It's not complimentary. And it is borderline offensive. Also it's a sure fire way to get your ass sat on.

"What gave you the idea that this would be okay? The entire hotel can hear you right now. And it's a really crappy song."

"You only think that because you didn't get to hear the best part. It holds the whole melody together. Let me play a little of it for you."

Before he can get to his guitar, I reach down and grab his arm. "Just go to your room. We've had enough problems from your group to last us a life time. Just go to your room and I won't break your guitar."

Even I have to admit that I should probably get fired for half the things that come out of my mouth. But they are going to cut me some slack. I've gone two weeks without a day off and, even more disturbing, my life has become a fucking Reba McEntire song.

***

Day Fifteen

In about nine minutes, I will be out of here. I won't have to think about this place for a blissful eighteen hours. What's ever better is when I come back tonight, the children will be gone. They will fly back to whatever corner of hell they came from and I won't ever have to help them again. Nothing is going to darken my day, not even the fact that Doogie just walked through the door.

I have even decided to celebrate by doing my own version of the White Boy Dance, the VERY White Boy Dance. It is kind of what you would imagine a seizure would look like if it were set to music. That's why it only comes out on special occasions.

The first group of kids to check out is walking up to the front desk. My face is doing something most unnatural, smiling without being forced. It makes me happy that the next time I see them it will be in hell where I will be aiding in making their afterlives miserable. (VIP Platinum seats, baby. I got the good rock.)

146

Doogie's walking to the front desk while I'm finishing up with the brats. This is good. I might be able to ditch him here at the front desk and get a three minute head start on my big eighteen hours. Doogie can wait here for a couple of minutes for the day agent to get here. It might not kill him to do a little bit of work.

"Sean, we have a bit of a problem."

"Correction. You've got a bit of a problem. Sean is going home and crawling in bed. There's no problem with that." Trust me when I say that the white boy dancing is getting worse. Arms are involved as well as the shaking of a nonexistent booty. (A nega booty if you will.)

"Jannelle called in sick. We had asked Derek to be here at six but he didn't show up and no one can get in touch with him."

"And this affects me how?" The white boy dance is losing some of its passion because I know exactly what he's about to say.

"We were hoping that you could do us a favor."

"I'm sorry, but I'm fifteen days into the last favor you asked me to do." Am I mistaken about my job title? I don't recall signing up for the position of Hotel's Bitch. As much as I might hide it with my sparkling personality, I don't really like this place that much. (Shocking, I know.)

"We just need you to stay until we can get someone else up here. It should only take about an hour or so."

"Then why can't you do it? Why should I give up any more of my time off because you can't seem to hire people who will show up on time?" This coming from the person who, two nights ago, sat in his car, eating a Double Whopper just to makes sure that he was fifteen minutes late. (I was pissed off and hungry.) "And who is this 'we' you keep talking about. You aren't a Borg. (Star Trek geek, Holla!)"

Doogie gives me some lame ass excuse about having some paperwork that has to be completed today. He knows I'm going to say yes because eventually I will realize that I need the money and extra hours equal more overtime. And I hate him for knowing that.

"Just so you know, when we're in hell, I'm throwing rocks at you too."

***

Day Fifteen 12:00 P.M.

So, that person "they" were supposed to get to relieve me after only an extra hour never showed up. I'm highly suspicious that there was no phone call made at all. I can't prove that to be true, but if I ever do, then Doogie better watch himself. He only thinks people make fun of his hair now. Wait until I'm through with it.

148

I've been calling Doogie every five to seven minutes to give him updates on how much I hate him at any given moment. My mood varies from blind rage to murderous contempt. It really just depends on the minute.

All pretense of politeness and any trace of a smile have been wiped from me. I don't care if these people think I'm rude. It has been five extra hours. I'm cranky. And I have been craving a hamburger since eight o'clock. Doogie won't even come outside long enough for me to smoke a cigarette. That certainly isn't helping my current attitude situation.

"We really enjoyed our stay. I hope they let us come back next year." The woman says this as she completely ignores the five children running around and throwing things at each other.

"I'm counting the minutes." I figure that is better than saying, "I hate you, your children, and your entire convention. Please get lost in the Bermuda Triangle on your way home." That would be harsh, wouldn't it?

I dial the back office. "I want a cigarette. Are you finished your paperwork yet?"

"No. I'm trying to get it done as fast as possible, but it is hard with the phone ringing every few minutes." Oh, he wants to get snappy with me, does he?

"Imagine how hard it would be if you had to work the front desk while doing it."

Now that got his attention. "It shouldn't be too much longer before someone comes to relieve you."

"That's what you said three hours ago. Excuse me if I don't put a whole lot of faith in that." The overtime really isn't worth all this. I could be in bed right now having sweet dreams about Doogie being tied to a railroad track. The only bonus is that I just watched the last of the kids leave the hotel.

Working this late into the day has taught me a very valuable lesson. There is a very good reason that I work the overnight shift. As many people as I have to deal with, there are five times more stupid people during the day. The lobby is full of people making an insane amount of noise. And then there is the whole sun thing. Me and the sun are not on good terms. (I prefer artificial light.)

"Just so you know, I'm checking myself into a room when I get off." I'm well aware that this is what Tanya got fired for, but I dare him to say something. As much as I don't like the idea of staying here, especially since I know the housekeeping staff, I'm not about to drive across town in afternoon traffic just to turn around and drive back a couple of hours later.

"I'll block a room for you."

It really does amaze me how a bitchy attitude will get me what I want.

***

Day Fifteen 3:00 P.M.

I am still here and getting more pissed off by the minute. There is a frown permanently plastered on my face. Doogie hasn't come out of the back office in an hour because the last time he did I yelled at him for bugging me. Really, if he wasn't there to let me go home, he served no purpose in my life.

But, it's three o'clock now and the afternoon shift should be here any second. Philip is working tonight and he is never late. (Which is why I have to love him instead of hating him because he's skinny. Dammit.) That's exactly what I need because, if I have to spend one more minute at the front desk, I might lose my mind. And I really need to get upstairs and take a shower. After sixteen hours, I'm starting to smell really funky.

Doogie thought he was being cute when he blocked a room for me. I guess he assumed that I didn't know how to use the computer so I wouldn't be able to see which room he put me in. But I'm not an idiot and I can see that he blocked a non-smoking room with double beds for me. That's really not going to work. The least he could give me is a king bed to sleep in and somewhere I can chain smoke.

151

So I change the room knowing damn well that Doogie won't look at it again. He thinks he's so smart.

"What are you still doing here?" I never thought I would be as happy to see another human being as I am to see Philip walking behind the front desk. Finally, I can stop talking to the guests. I don't have to pretend to care about their problems. The toilet paper in your bathroom isn't hanging in the right direction? Tell it to Philip.

"The morning shift never showed up and Doogie couldn't find anyone to come in. And, heaven forbid, he actually work the front desk himself."

"He should have called me. I've been sitting on my ass all day watching courtroom shows. I would have come in early if I had known you've been working all this time."

Oh yes. Doogie is going to die. Painfully. There may or may not be a crocodile involved in this plan. I knew he was yanking me all day with that bullshit about someone coming to take my place. I am so going to shave half his hair off so it looks like he only has one butt cheek on his head.

I grab my stuff and storm into the back office. There I find Doogie sitting at a very empty desk. He quickly closes a window on his computer that looks suspiciously like solitaire. He must be exhausted. He's obviously been working his ass off back here. I should really be ashamed of myself for complaining so much when he's been buried with work.

"So where's this urgent paperwork?"

"I just finished it. I was about to go outside to let you go, but Philip showed up."

"Convenient."

I don't want to talk to him anymore. All the rage that I felt walking back here and my desire to knock him upside his head with my cash drawer is just buried. I just want to go to sleep. Getting arrested for homicide would only postpone me getting in bed. (It would totally be justifiable though.)

I'm counting my cash drawer with my back to Doogie and doing my best to try to make his head explode with the untapped potential of my mind. Grace is sitting at her desk doing her best to ignore the fact that there is some major tension in the room.

"Sean?" Learning to keep his mouth shut is a skill that Doogie has never been taught.

"I'm not speaking to you right now. Something might slip out of my mouth and I'll get fired."

Grace clears her throat behind us. I don't know if that is meant to tell me to watch myself or to stifle a laugh. Either way it doesn't matter because I'm within my rights not to be speaking to that ass monkey right now.

"Sean, I need to know why you called to get an approval on someone's credit card for thirteen thousand dollars."

"I didn't."

"The computer says you are the one that checked the person in."

"Have I done or said anything in the past four months that gave you the impression that I'm stupid?" Grace snorts rather loudly from her desk. "The computer automatically calls for approval. Why would you think that I changed the computer's programming just so I could call and get thousands of dollars' worth of approval on someone's credit card? That is a completely unproductive use of my powers of hatefulness."

"I just want to make sure that you know the correct procedures on..."

"I have been working fifteen days straight. I'm just coming off a sixteen hour shift. I haven't had anything to eat since ten o'clock last night and that was a Slim Jim. (It's not meat. It's meat adjacent.) And I haven't had a cigarette since six thirty this morning. Do you really want to continue this conversation right now?"

Doogie sits quietly in his chair. For once, he has decided to do the smart thing and keep his mouth shut. I'm really not in the mood to have my job performance critiqued by a butt munch whose head looks like an ass.

"I'm going to bed now. Heaven help the person who wakes me up." I throw my cash drawer in the safe and storm out the office, leaving Doogie to look stupid in his chair. Grace, however, has her hand over her mouth and is doing her damnedest not to laugh.

***

Day Sixteen

For the past couple of nights, I've assumed that when day sixteen arrived, I would be in an outrageously bitchy mood. (One can see why I would easily come to this conclusion.) But I'm not. Strangely, I am almost pleasant to be around tonight. Jessie and I are having a kick ass good time. We've been signing Doogie up for transsexual porn newsletters using his work e-mail account. He should have an interesting inbox when he comes in.

Jessie understands my pain and has let me spend the majority of the night outside chain smoking. With the children gone, there isn't a whole lot for us to do. My presence here is quite unnecessary, but instead of giving me a much needed night off, Doogie is obviously punishing me. I'm sure this has everything to do with the conversation we had in the office. (Seriously. The man cannot let anything go.)

I have about three minutes left before I can go home. This time I've already called my relief to make sure that he is coming in on time. Derek was less than pleased when I woke him up at six o'clock. But if that's what it takes to get his ass in on time, then I'm sure as shit going to do it. I have no desire to have a repeat performance of yesterday.

Doogie has been nice enough to finally give me those four days off that I was supposed to get. I think this has more to do with the fact that he's probably tired of me arguing with him, or he's just sick of looking at my face, or a combination of the two. Whatever the reason, it doesn't matter. I'm finally getting my days off. Though four days off doesn't seem like enough time to recover from the past sixteen days of hell.

Jessie comes out of the back office with a look on her face that I know means trouble. "Derek just called to say that he's stuck in traffic. Strangely though, there were no sounds of traffic in the background. He obviously just woke up even after you called him. So he's going to be about thirty minutes late."

Severe hate. "Is he just physically incapable of coming to work on time? And who exactly is he blowing to still have a job here after the shit he pulled yesterday?" I need the kind of job security that only a well-placed blowjob can get me.

"You go on and go home. I'll work the desk until he gets here."

I do something extremely outside of my nature and hug Jessie. "You so just bought yourself like three days of me not making fun of you and your Cheeto grenades."

I run away from the desk before she has a chance to change her mind. I don't even bother counting my cash drawer before I throw it in the safe. The hotel will just have to wait a few days before they do a big deposit of thirty-seven dollars. Somehow I don't think anyone's paycheck is going to bounce.

As soon as I walk out the door, I strip off my ugly poo brown jacket. I haven't been able to do that all night because at some point a pen exploded all over my shirt without my knowing it. I look like a scene right out of CSI: Office Depot. But now that I'm off the clock, it is really the furthest thing from my mind. The only person who is going to see my shirt up close is the toll collector on my way home. Like I care if she judges me.

I walk out to my car that I parked on the street to make a speedy getaway and there it is, right on my windshield. A parking ticket. It has only been two minutes since the parking meters turned on and I've already got a ticket. This is usually the point where I become filled with righteous indignation and curse the meter maid's entire family. A pox on both your houses and all that. But I don't. I don't even roll my eyes. I take the parking ticket and get in my car.

Something is very wrong here. I think someone might be spiking my Coke with something. That or hell is freezing over.

***

Sixteen days without a day off is the devil. I figured it out and I worked the equivalent of 5.59 days. That's almost a week of my life that I will never get back. I could have used that time productively and learned a language or something. Not really, because I'm far too lazy for that, but the point is that I could have at least had the option.

Those sixteen days taught me a very valuable lesson. My soul has a price. Nine hundred forty-eight dollars exactly is how much it cost. I'm kind of disappointed because I though the price would be a little higher. An all-expense paid trip to Vegas or a date with Lance Bass. Something that would prove useful to me in the future.

About ten minutes after I deposited my check in the bank, a good fourth of it was handed over to the not-so-nice cashier at Target. I don't really call that useful. (Wonderful yes. Useful no.) But I decided to buy me some pretty for all my pain and suffering. Whoever said money can't buy you happiness is a fucking liar.

Request Denied

A Poem

To Our Guests

You suck

You really suck

You really really suck

I don't give a fuck

If you sleep in your truck

I'm afraid you're out of luck

Because I don't give a fuck

So go fuck a duck

You suck

(I obviously have too much time on my hands.)

***

"Dude, we are staaaaaarving. Where's a good place to get some nachos around here?"

"Um, dude, it's like four o'clock in the morning. I don't think nachos are on the menu anywhere." If it is I sure haven't found it because I would be eating that shit up. (I love me some anything covered in cheese.)

"But, DUDE, we are so hungry. We need nachos. Gooey nachos with lots of cheesy goodness." I have a very disturbing vision of a giant hookah set up in the middle of their room. We are going to have to steam clean the entire hall to get the smell of frat boy out of it. "Please, man. Fetch us some nachos."

"Sir, I really have no way of getting nachos at this time. And even if I did, I couldn't go fetch them because a) I can't leave the front desk; and b) I am not a golden retriever. You will just have to wait for normal nacho eating hours to get some." (Tell me to fetch something, indeed.)

I swear I didn't have a stroke or anything. And I'm not suffering from any delusions about what industry I work in. Ninety percent of the time I don't mind doing the guest request runs because they give me a chance to get away from the front desk and, more often than not, I sneak out for a cigarette when I'm finished. (I blame my diminished

160

lung capacity on people's inability to dry themselves off with one towel.) But I do believe there is a line that guest requests should never cross. I'm just not that customer service oriented.

The condom thing is one of those requests that I feel crosses the line by a lot. Especially seeing as I get this request approximately eighteen times a night. "We need some condoms up here really bad. The big kind if you know what I mean. Can you get them up here in about two minutes? I got this really hot chick up here."

Apparently, this gentleman believes I have lost the use of my eyes since he thinks that I didn't see him parading through the lobby with a great big hooker. The fishnets and the exposed nipple were dead giveaways on her status as a lady of the evening. "I'm sorry, but we don't have complimentary condoms."

"What do you mean?" Did I start speaking French without realizing it again? I've really got to stop doing that. It's very confusing to the guests. "This is the only hotel I've ever stayed at that doesn't offer free condoms. You would think that for the money I'm paying I could get a condom if I want one." I really want him to stop saying condom. He makes it sound so dirty.

"You would think for the money you're paying her she would supply the condoms."

The key to being a smart ass is knowing your audience. This guy is clearly drunk and horny. He won't remember to complain in the morning. And even if he does, he will be too worried about the fact that the whore ran off with his wallet and his wedding ring. Besides, chances are pretty good that he's not even listening to me right now.

"Guess I'm just going to have to ride it bareback then."

Eww. Was it absolutely necessary to share that bit of information? Is there something in my voice that screams it is acceptable to tell me details like that? Do I really seem like that open of a person?

"And I'm sure the bastard child your union will produce will grow up to become a financial drain on the economy."

Now I have to scrub my brain with bleach when I get home. That's just so time consuming. It would be much easier if the guests would keep disgusting information like that to themselves. And it would save me money on all that bleach.

For the most part, the guest request calls stop about two in the morning. After that I usually just have to bring someone a bottle of shampoo or a razor. With carry on restrictions for flights these days, the guests are lucky if they show up at the hotel still wearing their underwear. But tonight it seems that every five minutes someone needs something. I've grown tired of bringing people toilet paper

(Does everyone need to wipe their ass at the same time?), so I make Jessie do it.

Obviously, I didn't think this through because now I have to answer all the phone calls. "Good morning, Front Desk. This is Sean at your service." (HATE!)

"I've had a really rough day at work. My back is killing me. Could I get someone up here to give me a massage?"

"Um…no. There's no one here who can provide that service to you."

"You don't have a girl who can give messages at this hotel?"

"Not at this hour. Our masseuse is only on call until nine o'clock."

"Well, I need someone to come give me a rubdown. I don't know if I am going to be able to get any sleep with my back tangled in knots."

"I'm sorry about that, but it is four-thirty in the morning."

"What about you? Can't you come up here and give me a massage? I'll pay you."

No! He! Didn't! (Imagine a neck roll, if you must.) "Sir, I am so not a hooker."

"Wait. Hold on. I didn't say you were." He's not going to back himself out of this one.

"But you did just offer me money to come upstairs and touch you. This is basically implying that I am a hooker.

163

(Not really, but in my warped logic it is.) I don't appreciate that. And you are very lucky I don't report you to my manager and have you escorted from the hotel. Please do not call the front desk again."

Now if only I could tell the same thing to the other five hundred eighty-six rooms here tonight.

***

"Yes, ma'am, I am absolutely positive that there is no way that anyone will open the jewelry shop for you right now. The necklace will be there in the morning." It's fake anyway. There isn't a thing in that jewelry shop that is real and that includes that woman who runs it. She seriously looks like a washed out version of Milla Jovovitch's character in Zoolander. Nothing in the shop is worth anyone's time. That's why no one wants the free gift certificates that Doogie wants me to pass out to every guest. (I'm positive that is the reason and that it has absolutely nothing to do with that fact that I tell everyone that the jewelry is tacky and the shop is frequented by whores.)

And seriously, how much money do you have that you just wake up at two a.m. with a craving for necklace shopping?

Tonight I'm busy. Not with my job or anything, but with something even more important. I am putting together an application to be one of my minions. I have decided that my life will not be complete if I don't get me some minions and quickly. There is a lot of negativity to be spread throughout the world and I can't be expected to do it all myself.

Here's what I've come up with so far:

Application for Minionship
(Feel free to fill this out at home)

1) Name:

2) Sex:

3) Age: (We do not discriminate against age. We feel that all ages can benefit from the joys of being a bitch. But we must ask.)

4) On a scale of one to ten, how would you rate your own bitchiness?

5) On this same scale, how would others rate your bitchiness?

6) Duties of this position include, but are not limited to: extreme rage, random acts of hating on people, drive-by judgings, and overall acting superior to just about everyone. Do you feel like you can perform these duties?

7) Are you physically able to sit on your ass for hours at a time and bitch and moan about the world around you?

8) If you could be any character on Grey's Anatomy, who would you be?

9) Would you consider yourself a peppy person more than 3.5% of the time? (Note: Answering yes to this question automatically disqualifies you from minionship. I allow for 3.5% because everyone slips a little.)

10) This position may require you to sexually harass the cute office boys in underwear. Do you feel you are up to this challenge?

11) Pick one: A bowl of mixed fruits and berries or a thick slice of
cheesecake dripping in chocolate sauce.

12) Have you ever, in all your Knot's Landing glory, full on bitchslapped someone? Bonus points if you were wearing a big floppy hat when you did it.

13) In your opinion, what makes a better weapon: A shank crafted out of weave and Lee Press On Nails or a Stiletto heel?

14) When is the last time you laughed so hard you snorted?

15) If you could slap the shit out of anyone in the world, who would it be?

16) Sometimes I am far too lazy to do things for myself. Would you be willing to fetch me shit upon command?

17) Who is your favorite member of N'sync? (Anyone who knows me better know the answer to this question.)

18) Would you rather be an indestructible cheerleader or a crazy psycho bitch with multiple personalities who never washes her hair?

19) Practice Test: You and your best friend are sitting down, enjoying a Venti Mocha Frappuccino with a double shot of espresso, when this skanky woman walks past you in a tiny skirt of Paris Hilton proportions and a couple of rolls of belly fat hanging out from her halter top. What do you do? WHAT DO YOU DO?

20) In as few words as possible, (because I'm all about the lazy) explain why you would make a good minion.

I think I can generate some interest in my army of bitterness. I can imagine us sitting around in bars, me sending minions to fetch me colorful drinks, and talking smack about the people sitting around us. Everyone will be gathered around me, awaiting my orders to go spread out and judge. Then many hours later, after we have been kicked out of several bars, we will roam around the streets and question the hookers' choices in fashion. (Fishnets and hot pink tube tops do not go together. No no.) And then, me and my posse will go around giving hookers advice on the "Sometimes more is more" philosophy of clothing. After that…

I swear this phone will not leave me alone. Don't these people realize that, without me, my minions will be leaderless? There will be no one to guide them through to tough roads of bitchy. (Think of the minions!)

"I'm going to be leaving in a couple of hours, and I am trying to get packed up. I need you to send some dry ice to my room."

Is this woman drunk? Because this would really be one of those funny drunk requests that I could write about in my blog. She didn't slur her words or anything. But there's no way that this woman can be sober and calling me in the middle of the night for dry ice.

"We don't have any dry ice, ma'am?"

"How do you not have any dry ice?"

Why does everyone ask that question like it is the most absurd thing they have ever heard? Sure, if we were out of towels or shampoo, I would agree with that. But dry ice? Really? "It's not something that we really keep in stock. Why would we keep a surplus of dry ice on hand? You are the first person to ever request that."

"Where can I get some?"

"I don't know. I don't even know where you would find dry ice in the first place, much less at two thirty in the morning. You might want to wait until the morning when someone can direct you to where you can buy some."

"I can't wait until the morning. This has to be done tonight. I need to get this package ready for FedEx to pick up before I leave at five."

What could possibly be so important that it can't wait a couple hours? Since I don't really care, I'm not going to bother asking. "I'm sorry, ma'am, but I can't help you with that."

"You really shouldn't advertise yourselves as a full service hotel then."

"We don't because we're not."

"Well I'm a guest here and I need help. You need to find a way for me to get some dry ice so that I can ship my titty milk back home."

Titty milk? Gross. How could she possibly think that that term was acceptable and/or appropriate? I mean have some class. I know we aren't the classiest place in the world, but it's not like we're the Hilton or anything.

"I really have no desire to hear that. So, since there isn't anything I can do for you, I'm going to let you go. Good luck with that."

Okay, I know it's hard to tell over the phone, but I am a man. There are some mysteries that I am just never going to know. Boobs are right on the top of that list. I don't get them and I really don't want to. I mean I was under the impression that you didn't run out of breast milk. So what's the harm in throwing away a couple bottles of it? Are the breasts really going to shrivel up from lack of milk, dooming the poor child to a life of starvation? (Like I said, no boobies for me. I have no idea.)

And I have a hard time believing that she will be able to FedEx breast milk. With the stringent traveling policies, people can't even fly with toothpaste. Won't a box full of breast milk with no baby around look a little suspicious?

What pisses me off the most about this is that this woman has now and forever burned the term titty milk in my memory. And for that she must be destroyed.

Trying to push that phrase into the back part of my mind where I store things that are better left forgotten (like trying to explain to my mom what a MILF is. Twice because she forgot the first time), I continue to work on my minion application. Now I need them faster than ever if I am going to dispatch them to do horrible things to this woman and her titty milk.

RING!

"Can I get a couple extra towels up here in room 1411?"

Sure, why not. "I'll bring them right up, sir." (See, I can actually be polite when I want to be. Or when I've been

171

called into the office because a secret shopper says that I come off 'grumpy'.)

I decide to have my cigarette before doing this guest request run. Usually I would wait until after, but the guy sounded pretty awake so I figure he can wait a few minutes for his towels. And what kind of crisis is he going to have that he will absolutely, positively need these towels right away. Besides my smoking comes first. (It may be killing me, but it's keeping other people alive.)

Since my nicotine levels are just shy of overdose, I'm feeling pretty good. Not quite up to smiling without being forced to, but I'm in an okay mood. The guests haven't been too annoying tonight. Most of them are leaving me alone and the ones who are calling are being halfway nice, except titty milk woman. My attitude seems to improve when I don't have to contemplate what evil I can commit against the guest.

Armed with fresh towels, I walk down the hall to room 1411. He sounded like a nice guy so I might even get myself a tip out of this run. I like it when they tip because that means that I will have enough cash to take the toll road home and won't have to face all the crazies on the interstate. (Or have to steal out of my cash drawer for the money.)

I knock on the door and can hear him moving around in there. I don't mind waiting a few minutes. It's a good thing

I stopped for that cigarette or this would not be the case. But I don't think any amount of cigarettes could have prepared me for what happens when he opens the door.

He's standing there holding the door open and he is naked. Nude. In his birthday suit. Letting it all hang out.

I can't speak for the rest of the world, but I know that I am never expecting someone to open a door and find them naked. It's just not really something you can prepare for. You have to know it's coming for it not to be a complete shock. And there is no way you can hide the look on your face. It is also doubly hard to do so when the naked person in front of you is not attractive at all.

"Hey. Thanks, man."

I don't say a word, just stare in shock as I hand him the towels and he passes me a five dollar bill. (So not worth the damage done to my retinas.) I mean to start walking away, but I can't. I can't move a muscle. And worse yet, I can't stop looking at it. You know how you are driving along and you see a horrific accident and you know you should look away, but you can't. That's how this is. I don't want to look at it, but my eyes are immediately drawn to that spot.

"You okay?"

"You're naked." (Never underestimate my powers to state the obvious.)

"Yeah. It's the middle of the night. There's nothing wrong with being naked." He shifts his weight from one foot to the other.

Oh! It moved! Why can't I walk away? Run, Sean, run. Run and don't look back.

"You called me and ask me to come up here. So you knew that someone would be knocking on your door. You didn't even think about putting some pants on?"

"I didn't know who would be coming up here. It could have been a hot looking woman and she might have liked what she saw. Maybe I could have gotten some."

"That's gross."

Apparently that is what it takes to break the hypnotic effect of his not cute naked body. I force myself to walk away and not jump over the railing to get away as fast as possible. I really don't want to leave this guy with the impression that his naked body leads people to suicide. That would be rude.

"Hey. If you see any hot girls down in the lobby that look like they are in the mood, send them up here."

I think that totally calls for another cigarette.

***

Tonight has been a rather calm night, with the exception of Hillbilly Jim and his sidekick White Trash

174

Joe. They came in about one thirty talking about how they were "plumb tuckered out" from all the driving they had to do. I didn't really care but since we are a hotel I gave them a room and sent them on their way.

Jessie and I are using our time wisely. We're taking turns rifling through Doogie's drawers looking for shit to make fun of him about. I found a couple of customer service surveys that were faxed over from the corporate office. Usually these are posted on the walls so that we can see what the customers say we did wrong while checking them in. The really bad ones are usually highlighted and put on display to shame the agent who gave such horrible service. The exception is with reviews that report Doogie for bad performance. Those get hidden in his desk.

Not anymore. I just have to find a way to post these all over the hotel without him knowing I did it. He already hates me. And I've already had a little meeting about how my attitude has a tendency to be on the bad side. I don't really need to give him any more ammunition against me. As it is, he's come very close to reading my various Death for Doogie plans. (Perhaps I shouldn't have left them sitting on the front desk, but Philip found them amusing.)

That is pretty much how Jessie and I spend our nights. When we aren't actively looking for things to make fun of Doogie about, I'm writing about the things that we've already found for my blog. Thanks to Jen Lancaster I now have random people throughout the country hating on Doogie. That makes all the stupid shit he does worth it.

The phone rings and I can see from the caller ID that it's room 1930 calling. This is not good because I know this is the room that I just put Hillbilly Jim in. I just knew that I hadn't heard the last of them.

"We've got a big problem up here. Me and my buddy here have been on the road since eight o'clock this morning. You know how things can get when you've been stuck in a car for so long. It's hot, you get all sweaty, and certain things come up." I know where this is going and I'm not at all wanting to hear it. "I'm sure you can imagine how horny we are." La la la. Not listening. "We need you to call up one of the escort services and get us a couple women. I'd like a blonde and my buddy would like a redhead. Our price range is between two and three hundred dollars. And make sure they have big tits."

I'm trying to figure out at what point during the entire time I was checking them in did they see me decked out in a big pimp suit with a floppy purple hat with fur on the brim. I don't think I mistakenly wore my boots with fish in the heels tonight.

"I'm not a pimp, sir."

"I know that, but I thought you could help us out. Surely, you have connections and can get us some hot chicks."

I am well aware that the rooms are a tad bit overpriced. Let's just say that if it weren't for the fact that I get an employee discount, there is no way in hell that I would be paying our rates. While I know that we overcharge people to stay here, hooker fetching is not included in the price. And why would anyone assume that I have connections in the whoring industry?

"I don't have connections, sir. Prostitution is illegal and I don't really care enough about you and the other guests to break the law for you."

"You mean to tell me that you don't know at least one girl who would come over and give us a ride. I don't think that's true. You don't understand how bad we need it. We got this porn playing in here and we are all worked up. Come on, help us out."

"Sir, I am not going to call a hooker for you. That is not my job. If you are that worked up and can't call your own hooker, then I suggest you look over at your buddy for some help."

"We're not like that, man. We need some pussy and you need to find us some."

"Yeah. I'll get right on that."

Really? Are there hotels out there that offer these services to random hillbillies? If there are I would really like a list of them so that I can make sure that I never apply for a job there. Though I would consider filling out an

177

application for Doogie. He is totally the type of kiss ass who would do a hooker hunt for a drunk hillbilly.

I'm Not Making

Employee of the Month

Sean's 90 Day Evaluation

(Answers are given on a scale from 1-5. 5 is the highest and 1 is the lowest. Please share these answers with employee when completed.)

1) How well does employee communicate with other employees? 3

2) Does employee work well without being supervised? 4

3) Is employee accurate in his/her assigned tasks? 5

4) Does employee follow the company dress code as stated in The Hotel employee handbook? 5

5) Does employee follow all safety codes when working in and out of his/her area? 5

6) Does employee show proficient knowledge of all equipment (i.e. computers, credit card machines, washer and dryer) that he/she needs to complete his/her job? 5

7) How would you rate employee's ability to interact with guests? 3

8) Does employee handle disputes between guests and/or employees with respect? 3

9) Is employee capable of communicating comments, concerns, and complaints in a timely manner? 5

10) Overall, how would you rate employee's job performance? 4

(This section of the evaluation is to be completed by the employee after discussing the above portion.)

1) Is there anything that you would like to change about your working environment?

I think that CERTAIN members of management should be more concerned with addressing issues that arrive with the guests than standing over the employees' shoulders waiting for them to do something wrong. This is a completely inefficient use of time and not to mention rather annoying.

2) What are your career goals in the next five years?

I WANT TO OWN YOU!

What I would really like to know is who lit a joint and then decided to write this evaluation? And as much as it pisses Doogie off, I did surprisingly well on it. It may just be on technicalities that they had to give me a good score (They only asked if I was capable of communicating in a timely manner. They didn't say anything about how loudly I do it.), but I still got a good score. That's mainly the reason that I am not mentioning that this 90 day evaluation is about 47 days late.

Doogie found out about my blog. I'm not sure how he discovered it because he doesn't really seem like the Myspace type. In fact, if he actually has a profile, I am going to seriously consider deleting mine. I can't stand the thought of us having something in common.

Needless to say, he isn't too happy about this. I'm trying to figure out how this is supposed to be different from every other second of his life. (I assume it is hard to be happy when you have a stick permanently lodged up your ass.) He does not find my comments about his butt shaped head at all amusing. Which is total bullshit because everyone else who's read it finds it to not only be funny, but completely true.

I've been sitting in the back office with him for the past twenty minutes while he goes on and on about how he doesn't find my behavior to be professional. He's talking about how I should be written up for what I've done. Apparently I am supposed to be shaking in my shoes about a piece of paper that says I'm a bad boy. Besides I can't figure out what rule I broke. Last time I checked, talking shit about people wasn't a crime.

"I don't think you understand the seriousness of what you have done."

"You're right, I don't. You act like I've committed some heinous crime against humanity. All I did was make fun of some people."

He crosses his arms and tries to stare me down. He fails miserably because how exactly am I supposed to be intimidated when I'm expecting him to run out of the room any moment so he can complete a tricky surgery before his curfew? "Do you find that to be professional behavior?"

"Let me ask you something. Did I slap the homo who accused me of molesting his dog? No. I call that a damn good job of professionalism."

He makes some sort of grunting noise that is supposed to signify that I'm just not "getting it". He always does that whenever he doesn't have a response to whatever I say, so he does it rather often. This makes me seriously question his management skills. If he can't keep up with one smart ass, then what chance does he have out there with all the really mean people?

"I had a feeling that you wouldn't understand the seriousness of your actions, so I asked Leeland to come and handle this situation."

Okay. That has me a little worried, but I will not show that to Doogie. Leeland is the Front of House Manager, encompassing all visible parts of the hotel. He's Doogie's boss. He's everyone's boss. I've met him a couple of times, but we've never really talked that much. He's this stern looking black guy who never smiles and he scares me a little. So I think I am pretty much in deep shit now. Leeland is not going to see the humor in my work, even though I still don't know what rule I've broken.

Leeland walks in the office and I'm pretty much shitting on myself. I work very hard to keep my face straight because I refuse to give Doogie the satisfaction of knowing that he's got me scared.

For another ten minutes, I sit in my chair and listen to Doogie give a full account on all the reasons that I am going straight to hell. Where do I get the nerve to talk about stupid people in such a derogatory manner? It may just be wishful thinking, but I think Leeland looks a tad bit annoyed with Doogie. Could this play in my favor?

"Okay. Just let me read what you are talking about."

Doogie pulls up one of my blog entries. I can see it is one of the ones that I wrote about those ill-conceived children that were here for their church retreat. Yeah. That could get me in serious trouble. I said some pretty awful things about those kids. Doogie obviously did his research before calling this little meeting. (Bonus points for premeditated evil.)

The entire time Leeland reads, Doogie sits across from me giving me the evil eye. What he doesn't realize is that I was raised with two brothers, so I am much better at the whole staring someone down thing. I've had years of practice. Just because I'm scared of Leeland's reaction doesn't mean for one second that I'm afraid of Doogie. He can still totally suck it.

Leeland spins around in his chair with a stern look in his eyes. It is the kind of look that would make a stronger man lose control of his bladder. "Did you write this?"

"Yes, sir." Dammit. Now I sound like a fifth grader in the principal's office. That's another thing I am going to have to destroy Doogie for. (Life was so simple when I could just blame everything on Meredith Grey.)

Without any kind of warning, Leeland starts laughing. It's a deep laugh that doesn't sound natural. I've never seen Leeland laugh before and it is a rather scary sight coming from someone who I didn't even know could smile. Doogie looks pissed that Leeland is laughing and not immediately giving me the reprimand that he feels I so deserve. It's hard, but I am stopping myself from jumping up and shaking my ass in Doogie's face. That would not be a wise move when I am so close to winning this little battle.

"You certainly have a unique take on our guests." He's still laughing, but just a little bit. It's more like a giggle, which is even creepier. "Just change the names so we don't have any problems."

"I've only used a man's real name once and that was because he burped in my face. (Pop a mint, man.) I thought that was more than acceptable." I couldn't just leave well

185

enough alone, could I? No! I had to go and open my big, fat mouth even though I'm not in any trouble. Now Leeland is going to detach his jaw and swallow me whole. Stupid.

Leeland thinks this over for a couple of seconds. "Fair enough."

The look on Doogie's face is beyond priceless. I really wish that I would have thought to bring a camera to work so I could immortalize this moment. I want to be able to remember it forever and ever but my short term memory is shot to shit from hours and hours of watching the Game Show Network. Damn. Maybe I could replace 'titty milk' with this image in my mind with the caption 'My Triumph Over Doogie' or 'Doogie Can Suck On It'.

"Sean, please go back to the front desk. I want to have a conversation with Doogie for a few minutes."

I keep careful control over myself, so I don't skip out of the office in glee, singing, "Doogie's in trouble. Doogie's in trouble." Even I know when to quit when I'm ahead. (Sometimes.)

As the door is closing, I can't help but hear part of the conversation going on in the office. (I'm sure that me all but sticking my head in the room had nothing to do with that.) "What do you think you're doing? I have more important things to do than worry about what someone is writing…"

Oh fuck it.

"Doogie's in trouble. Doogie's in trouble."

I get the feeling that Karma has taken a vacation.

***

There are big changes happening at the front desk. It's been almost a month since Tanya got fired and they've finally hired someone to take over her position. It turned out to be a lot harder than they thought it was going to be. It took a while but they have finally realized that the majority of the people at the front desk would rather have root canals than take the position. All the bullshit we put up with is not really worth the extra fifty cents an hour. (At the end of the night, I walk away with four more dollars than everyone else. Watch out Vegas. High roller coming through.)

Jessie informed me last week that there has been serious talk of Doogie taking over the shift for a while. As you can imagine this idea was met with a resounding, "OH, HELL NO!" from me. A person on the 18th floor may have called to complain about a loud noise coming from the lobby. Just think of the loud noises that would be made if Doogie and I had to spend all night together. I think not.

Surprisingly enough, they listened to me. I guess after our little meeting with Leeland, he did not think that it was wise to put the two of us together. Bloodshed would ensue

187

and then he would lose two employees. Doogie would certainly be dead and I would be carted off to jail for bludgeoning him with a three hole punch. (And don't think I won't find the first huge guy named Tiny I see and become his bitch on my first day.)

Earlier this week, Leeland bribed Aden to come back to the overnight shift as the manager. I am all for this decision. I enjoy working with Aden, especially when she talks shit about people in broken English. When they first offered her the job, she flat out refused. Rumor has it that she laughed in their faces and walked out of the room. I would have done the same thing, but they didn't ask me. (Go figure.)

Apparently, they offered her more money and guaranteed weekends off to get her to take the job. Personally, I don't trust them for a second. They will probably give her the first weekend off and then BAM! they'll have her working every single one of them along with me. (I have yet to find who I have to blow to get weekends off.)

So starting tonight, Aden and I will be working together again. I'm really happy about this because as much as I love working with Grace, she's kind of boring. She doesn't find the same joy in talking merciless smack about people. Grace is more of the good kind of worker. She hates conflicts with the guests so she gives them whatever they want. It's like she's a Stepford manager.

I'll still get to work with Jessie two nights a week so we will still be able to do our covert Doogie harassing. I've never quite gotten the story on what he did to piss her off so bad, but I'm sure it was something stupid. Most of the things Doogie does are stupid, so it doesn't really surprise me.

It's been kind of slow tonight so I've been printing out some of my blog entries to let Aden read them. She hasn't stopped laughing for thirty minutes. I'm not going to lie, I do not think I'm very funny, so when someone laughs at something I say or write, it makes me feel good. And when Aden lets out a huge snort, let's just say that it warmed my icy heart for a few seconds.

"Oh, Sean, you really crack me down."

I love her and her blatant disregard for American slang. I know that she has been in this country for a while because her English really isn't too bad. I've never had any trouble understanding what she is trying to say. Granted some of the guests do because they are too lazy to listen, but she can get her point across quite well. There are just certain phrases that she can't get out right.

While reading one of my entries, she laughs out loud and says, "This did not happen. I don't believe you. You are pulling my hair."

It's for this and many other reasons that I want to put her in my pocket and take her home. I can tell that she is the type of person that I want to go to bars with and make fun of the slutty girls. She could be my head minion. I can just imagine all the trouble that we are going to get into on this shift.

It beats working with Doogie though.

***

Christmas time is here and it kind of sucks. I'm not a big fan of the holidays because (I'm sure this comes as a surprise) I would much rather stay in bed than do all the holiday cheer crap. Around this time of year, I usually stock up on DVDs because of the mass influx of holiday themed movies and TV shows. I mean they are all the same. Some woman who has turned her back on the true meaning of Christmas and become a Grinchette goes on a business trip but her car breaks down in some Podunk town where it will take two weeks to fix because they have to order the part and while she's waiting she falls in love with a lumberjack or tree or something and gets the greatest present of all, a heart. (Vomit.)

Call me Scrooge, but there are only so many times that I can watch A Christmas Story before I want to puke. (I reached that point when I was about seven.) There are very few holiday movies that I can stand. (A Very Brady Christmas is about the only one. Shut. Up.) I didn't get my movie stash this year because I'm rather low on the fundage. My car is a demanding bitch. So I will have to make due with watching one of 172 other DVDs that I already own. (The horror!)

In a move that is quite unlike me, I have decided to try to find some things that I should be grateful for this year. This is proving to be a lot harder than I anticipated. In an hour all I've been able to come up with is that I am thankful for the existence of the Double Gulp at 7-11. Though I am not grateful for the fact that I have to drive all the way to Dallas to get one. (So almost worth it.)

The list of things that are pissing me off during this holiday season is growing at a rather rapid pace though. Like the fact that yesterday I broke my toe. (I will go to my grave saying that that bed jumped in my way.) You don't really realize how much you need your toes until one of them is broken and you can't use any of them. So now I have to walk around the hotel looking like an idiot and have someone stop me every five seconds to ask me what's wrong. "Oh, nothing. I just woke up and decided it would be fun to walk around like a jackass for a while." (Really, people, if I actually wanted you to know I would have bitched about it to you already. Now leave me the hell alone.)

A close second on this list is, of course, Doogie. He's usually always number one, but I feel that broken bones piss me off more. This time it isn't so much what he's done to anger me, it's more that he's my Secret Santa. (Fuck that secret. I want to know.) I can only imagine what he is going to get me. I'm betting on an attitude adjustment.

I hate doing Secret Santa. I don't really want to buy anything for my co-workers. (Except Philip. I would buy him a cheeseburger.) Especially since we are just going to buy each other gift cards to the same damn place. I'll just spend my money there and cut out the middle man. But knowing that Doogie picked my name sort of makes me wish I hadn't filled out my list with various methods of death for him. Anyone else would have found it funny, but Doogie had to blow it all out of proportion. After reading my blog, I wouldn't think he'd be surprised. He's such a baby.

And he's been working my nerves for the past two hours. He should have left already, but he's still here "working". Talking on the phone and shopping for cars online only counts as work if it's me doing it. This is that "important paperwork" bullshit all over again. And to top it off, he won't shut the fuck up.

"This isn't right. I had to work Thanksgiving and now they're making me work Christmas too. And Leeland just told me that I am going to have to work New Year's Eve

192

and New Year's Day as well." (I heart Leeland.) Why he's bitching about all this to me is a mystery? He can't honestly think that I am going to be very sympathetic towards him. "It's just not fair. How am I supposed to have any kind of a life? I had planned to take my girlfriend out for New Year's. It was going to be very romantic and…"

"Shut up." I somehow make these two words have eight syllables between them.

Doogie looks stunned. It has never been a secret that I don't like him, but I've never come right out and told him to shut up before. There's always been that line that I try not to cross. Sure I talk back to him all the time, but I've never been downright disrespectful. (Trust me, I haven't.) Truth be told though, it gives me warm fuzzies. Besides, his voice is giving me an ear infection.

"You act like you're the only one who has to work crappy hours. I had to work Thanksgiving. You are making me work Christmas. And you've already told me that I am required to work New Year's. And that's not to mention the sixteen days in a row that I worked for you not long ago or all the other overtime that I pull. On the overnight shift. With a broken toe. (Barefoot. In the snow. For five miles! Uphill in both directions!) How am I supposed to have a life? I have to sleep all day so I can stay awake all night to be here." He got me started now and I'm not really about to stop. "Besides, aren't you a manager? Doesn't being part of management mean that you have to work all sorts of crappy hours? Shouldn't you be the one to be there just in case someone messes up like you're always accusing us of doing?"

"Well, being in management should mean that I should be able to delegate responsibilities when I need to."

"No. Being in management means that you are in charge. You have to be here to manage things. See how those two words are kind of similar. It means that it is your responsibility to make sure things are running smoothly, not delegate it and make it someone else's job." (I've learned everything I know about management from Doogie. I always ask myself WWDD? What would Doogie do? I take that answer and do the complete opposite. Works wonders.)

Yeah. That shut him up real quick. He goes off to the back to sulk because he's been put in his place by a lowly front desk agent. (That's Night Auditor to you, biotch.) He doesn't really want to play the who-gets-screwed-over-worse-game with me because I will win and make him feel like an ass.

I just really can't take Doogie complaining. After five minutes he starts to sound like me and we just can't have that. There is only room for one chronic complainer here and that is me. Basically because I am so much better at it than he is.

You know I probably shouldn't complain so much about my job. Where else could I actually talk to my manager that way and still have a job when it's over. Granted when I worked at the casino I said worse things to Rick on a nightly basis, but I was so good at my job that they didn't dare fire me. (I know that sounds rather conceited and you may be right but when I quit that job, they had to promote three people to take my place.)

And really? The look on his face was just lovely. I think I am going to consider that my real Christmas present from him. Merry Christmas to me!

***

Christmas is not at all like I expected it to be. I thought the hotel would be full of grouchy people who are pissed off because they have to spend the holiday in a hotel. (See: Thanksgiving.) But that's not what is happening at all.

It is Christmas Eve and the entire hotel has been rented out by this one company, whose name I don't know, to have a Christmas party of epic proportions. There are three different bands playing in different parts of the hotel. And we aren't talking cheap little cover bands. These are bands that I've even heard of. There are seven open bars scattered throughout the lobby. The whole building is just a clusterfuck of people.

The noise level is so loud that Jessie and I can't even talk to one another. And surprisingly that's okay with me. It's amazing how much noise you can tolerate when you don't have guests calling from random rooms to complain. Apparently the company made a condition that they would rent the hotel as long as no regular guests were allowed to stay there. I don't know what this company does but I want to work there. Especially since no one will tell me how much money they paid to do this. It's that top secret. (Which means I am dying to know.)

The only downside that I have seen so far is there is an overabundance of the tight jeans/cowboy hat combination going on. I am well aware that this is Texas and this kind of thing happens but there really should be a limit. Though I really shouldn't talk about the way other people dress because I think I am the only gay man in the world who was not blessed with a fashion sense, but I really shouldn't be able to read the label of your underwear through your pants. (Unless you're hot then that's okay because it gives me something to look at.)

But that is not the worst fashion choice that I've seen tonight. There are like five different people trying to pull off the upper body tuxedo/lower body tight jeans look. It doesn't work especially since some of them decided to add the cummerbund.

Though I am willing to look past their inability to dress themselves because they have all been really nice. You would think that in a large group of people like this there would be at least one asshole in the bunch. But no. They have all been rather well behaved. With the alcohol flowing as it has been, they have all moved into Happy Drunk and not Stupid Drunk, which is where I always run into trouble with them. One lady even gave me a five dollar tip for no reason whatsoever. If more people could just be Happy Drunk, I probably wouldn't be as mean as I am. (Anything's possible, right?)

Another cool thing about this party is that to make sure that everything goes okay, three of the managers are working late tonight. And Doogie isn't one of them. (He bitched and moaned enough to where Leeland gave him the day off out of sheer annoyance. At least I have the ability to be funny when I bitch about shit.) So that means that I can go up to each manager at random points in the night and ask to go have a cigarette break and they all think it's my first one of the night. I thoroughly enjoy getting paid to sit outside smoking cigarettes. Now if I could only turn that into a full-time job somehow.

Since there are no real guests in the hotel, there is absolutely nothing for me to do, except watch the party. I really wish I knew who these people were because I would really love to start spreading gossip about the girl who has her hands down some guy's pants on the dance floor. I'm sure everyone will be standing around the water cooler at work next week talking about that whore in accounting. (Aren't the whores always in accounting?)

"Are you havings funs?"

There is a drunk woman standing in front of me. She is holding onto the desk for dear life. I think if she lets go she is going to become intimately familiar with the floor. It's really strange to see her barely standing up because she's dressed so professionally, much more so than anyone else at this Christmas party. She is wearing this business casual suit and her hair is pulled into a tight bun. (If you are going to figuratively let your hair down, why don't you do it literally too?) This woman does not look like she would ordinarily be so hammered in a public place. But 'tis the season.

"Thish is a fucking fantashtic party. You shoulds be havin mores fun."

"Surprisingly, I am having fun. Even though I am at work."

"Work is shit!" This woman is so precious. I totally want to film her and post the video on YouTube. She could be the new internet sensation, Drunk Bun Lady.

"It can't be too bad. At least you work for a nice company that throws you a massive Christmas party." To prove my point, hundreds of streamers come flying over the railings of seven different floors and land on the big dance floor. (Seriously, I want to know how much money they spent on this party and how I can work for them. I don't care if they sell chemical weapons to third world countries.)

"Ish not that greats. I is ones of the vicsh preshidents of the company. The only reashon wes are throwshing thish party ish because we are doing masshive layoffses for New Years. But, SHHHHSHHHHSHHH! Don'ts tellsh anybody. Itsh a shurprise."

Why don't I ever get gossip like this when it can actually be of use to me? I'm not terrible enough to ruin the party by telling these people that they may not have a job in a few days. That's too much even for me. Dammit! Why couldn't these people be awful and obnoxious? Then I could use this information against them and hate on the whore from accounting. But they're not and I can't. This sucks.

But just so my night isn't a total loss, I run straight to Jessie to tell her that this whole thing is just a guilt party because they are going to can half the staff. There was a time in my life when I would have taken joy out of their misery no matter how nice they were. (I was just that big of an ass.) But ever since my unfair and totally unforgivable termination from the evil financial institution, I have a softer heart for people who are going to get fired. (Except for Autumn. That bitch had to go.) But that does not mean that I can't delight in a good piece of gossip, which is something we are so lacking in around here. (Doogie sucks. That's not gossip. That's scientific fact.)

Something that gets me is that with all the money that they are spending to rent out the hotel, couldn't they afford to not lay people off? And that's not to mention the money spent on alcohol, the decorations, the elaborate lighting, and the three bands which include one major country singer that I used to have a major crush on when I was younger. (Don't worry, Lance. He means nothing to me.) I can't even begin to imagine how much money it all costs. Surely, it is enough to fund payroll for at least a year. Maybe I don't want to work at this company after all.

But more importantly, I think someone is smoking pot somewhere in the lobby. With all these people here, I have no way of seeing who it is, but someone has to be because Jessie and I are getting a severe case of the munchies. It's two o'clock in the morning and our stomachs are growling. This is not normal behavior or a Taco Bell commercial, so that's the only explanation I have.

And this is not some wimpy ass hunger that a tiny ass bag of Doritos is going to cure. (The bag has like 6 chips in it. Cost: $3.48. Bend over please.) This calls for meat or some by-product of meat. And since my being at work is merely for show, Jessie has the wonderful idea of sending me out for food. This is a wonderful idea until everyone at the front desk, the hotel operator, the maintenance guy, and two guests who overhear us talking (I'm pretty sure they are the stoners) decide that they want food too. What was going to be a beautiful moment between me and a hamburger has been tarnished.

Now the only place that stays open this late in the general area is Jack in the Box and it's not in the best part of town. It's cool to go to if it is just going to be an in and out run, but not so much if it turns out to be a 65 dollar food run. I don't like to be sitting idle in a place where no one cares if you scream. (And just a note: The overnight workers at your local Jack in the Box do not enjoy working. They don't care if your order is right. Whatever it takes to get you out of their line so they can sit back down and watch T.V. (or porn as was my case), they are going to do it. And when you go through the drive-thru and order 65 dollars' worth of food, they are imagining you dead.)

Driving back to the hotel, I know it is going to be days before I can get the smell of pickles out of my car, but it is so worth it because there are three Jumbo Jacks and two orders of Bacon Cheddar Potato Wedges with my name on them. (YUM!!!)

I feel like Santa passing all this food out. The two guests that placed orders with me have disappeared, so I'm going to eat their food and keep their money. That's what they get for giving me a contact high. Merry Christmas to me!

***

Sixty nine thousand six hundred dollars. That's how much money they spent to rent out the hotel for one night. That's not even counting everything else. That's just for the hotel. (Going through Doogie's desk pays off.)

As nice as the party was, I think I would rather keep my job.

***

My toe is still broken and I am not at all happy about this. It pisses me off so much that I can't even be happy that Christmas and all the crap that comes with it is over. I've tried many different things so walking on it doesn't make me want to shoot myself in the foot, but I haven't had any luck. I've taken to wearing my favorite pair of shoes to work, which are really no more than fuzzy slippers. Doogie isn't thrilled with the idea.

"Those don't fall under the dress code. You aren't going to be able to wear them."

"Whoever came up with the dress code probably didn't have a person with a broken toe in mind. My dress shoes cut into my toe which makes it hurt worse which then makes me complain more. Besides, no one can see my feet behind the desk, so it's these shoes or no shoes."

He's even less thrilled with this option. (He really doesn't want to smell my feet.) He should just be glad that I haven't called in sick. Because whatever he might think, I am a responsible employee.

And really, my toe is just a hindrance to me now. There are big things happening in the world right now and I can't have my concentration split by a broken appendage. How else am I going to solve the mystery of how Ashlee Simpson became the not crazy Simpson sister? (If I were Jessica, I would die. I would just die.) Or discover what exactly is wrong with LiLo? (I so hate that name. Lilo is the name of a precocious little Hawaiian girl with a pet alien. It should never be associated with Lindsay Lohan.) Or gawk at the train wreck that is Britney Spears? (The poor brothers Federline. What's even worse is you know Sean Preston is going to be known as SPF for the rest of his life.) These are important issues and I will not have time to get to them if I have to limp around because I cannot bend my fucking toe.

And the arrival of the Rutgers's football team is not helping me at all. I've never really been one to follow the sports, but I did go to LSU, so I know how important college football is to the rest of the world. What I don't understand is why they have to be so damn loud? They are just staying here. We aren't hosting some fucking pep rally here. (I don't smell like team spirit.) Shouldn't they be resting or something?

I understand college students are going to party. (Hello. Went to LSU. It's not exactly known for its nuclear physics department.) But I've seen the schedule that these guys are going to have to live by for the next six days. If I were them, I wouldn't be worried about partying and screaming my head off. I would be more concerned about not dying. And on top of that, they can't do anything while they are here. No phone. No internet. No porn. What are they so excited about?

A man walks up to the front desk. I can only suspect he is the coach for the team, judging from the obscene amount of Rutgers's memorabilia plastered all over his body. (Subtlety has its finer points. Just because I choose not to use them does not mean they aren't there.) I'm seriously wanting to bet that this man is wearing some sort of Rutgers themed underwear.

"I need some help. I spoke this over with one of the managers who was here earlier. He said it was alright if I got someone who has a master key to come with me." That would be Doogie. Obviously it was just too much trouble to pass along that information before he left. This is just another thing I can add to the very long list of reasons to kill him. (Reason # 328: He gave me black socks as my Secret Santa gift. This was his way of telling me that I need to wear them to work instead of the white ones I've been wearing. Because so many people can see them.) "I just need someone to come with me so I can do bed checks for my players."

"Bed checks? Seriously? Aren't these people in college or something?"

"Yeah, but this is an important game coming up and that's how I run my team."

I'm not going to argue with him even though I think it is the stupidest thing I have ever heard. I went to boarding school for my last two years of high school, so I got an early start on my "college" experience. The most beautiful part about it was that there was none of this bedtime bullshit. Seeing as these guys are probably seniors, I would be pissed off if I was being told what time I had to go to bed. But then again, I'm sure these boys take the volleyball very seriously.

The team has three entire floors reserved especially for them. That's 96 rooms that we have to go check. That is not going to be fun to do when I can't bend my toe. Fuck these fucking football players right up their fucking asses.

Now there is a plus side to being stuck on bed check duty. As it turns out a good two-thirds of this team is really hot. And their coach is kind of a dick. Instead of knocking on the door, he instructs me to just open it without giving his players any kind of warning. That means that I am getting to see a lot of hot football players in various stages of undress. (A.K.A, a homo's dream come true.) Unfortunately, that also means I get to see the not so hot ones in their underwear as well. Small price to pay. Though I did see about five different guys wearing Rutgers themed underwear, so the odds that the coach is wearing them too just skyrocketed.

It takes exactly one hour and fifty-three minutes to do these bed checks. By minute five I was hating these people with an ungodly passion. My toe is hurting so bad that I am actually considering hacking it off with a butter knife I found on a discarded room service tray. I'm sure Lily would have loads of fun with that.

"Thanks for your help. I know it sounds kind of harsh giving grown men a bedtime, but you have to keep them in line so they play their best."

"Yeah. That's fascinating. Am I done, because I really need to get some ice on my toe?"

"Sure. We'll do this at the same time tomorrow."

"The anticipation may kill me."

I don't care how many hot guys I get to see in their underwear, it is so not worth this kind of agony. (From the amount I'm bitching, you'd swear I am walking around the hotel with a gaping stab wound in my chest. In my defense, my foot hurts, dammit!)

It's pretty obvious that Karma is back from vacation and she is hell bent on making me her bitch.

***

Judging from the level of noise in the lobby, I take it the team won their little racquetball match. Sure, I'm happy for them. It's always nice when there is a little more joy in the world. (I just threw up in my mouth a little.) But I don't understand why they are having the victory party here. We are not really set up for that kind of event and I do not have the proper attitude to attend.

And I really don't care how well the game went, I do not know how it justifies me having to wear this stupid cap to work. It really doesn't vibe with the quasi-suit that they make me wear. Besides, a red and black hat severely clashes with my poo brown uniform. It also gives the impression that I support this team. And I do not.

After four nights of doing their goddamn bed checks, I've had it with these people. Do you know what happens if one of the players isn't in his room at bed check time? We have to go find him. No matter where he is. "Why the hell can't I just stay here instead of walking all over the hotel to find someone who obviously has trouble telling time?"

"Because you have the key and what if I need to get into another room?" I hate this man and he hates me. At least we are on the same page.

I swear on more than one occasion we walked into a room and the guys in there were indulging in some "extracurricular activities". (I have no proof of this but there is just something about someone leaping across the room into his own bed at the sound of the door opening that makes one suspicious. And that is incredibly stupid because they knew exactly what time we would be coming.) And it wasn't even worth my time because they were so not the cute guys.

But now the celebration is in full blowout mode because all these people got drunk at the game. Alcohol and bloated middle aged men do not mix well together at football games. Their beer hazed minds give them delusions that they were actually responsible for the win somehow. (This is not the case.) And I've already heard several men's accounts of how this game reminded them of the time that they led their high school to victory in the championship game. (A la Al Bundy.) Those were the days. (And if they hadn't knocked up the head cheerleader in the back of their El Caminos, they could still be the days.)

The phone rings and I just know deep down in my heart that it is a noise complaint. How could it not be? I have the equivalent of an entire Mardi Gras parade stuffed in the

208

lobby. Someone, besides me, has got to be pissed off about this.

"Good evening…"

"Man, we are so fucking hungry. All that excitement at the game really worked up an appetite. We need to get some fucking food. Isn't there a McDonald's right down the street?" I do not enjoy being interrupted when I am answering the phone. It might be a stupid ass greeting, but I still like to get it out before I have some drunken moron yelling in my ear.

"Yes, there is a McDonald's right down the street but it is closed for the night."

"What do you mean it's closed?" Obviously my explanation was not clear enough. "How can it be closed?"

"I'm not exactly sure what the hours are for this one but I do know that it closes somewhere around ten."

"I can't believe this. I can't believe that a big hotel like this doesn't demand that places around you stay open to feed your guests."

I'm sorry, but I'm not a nine foot clown with a big red wig and weird yellow suit. How is it my fault that this McDonald's closes earlier than all the others? "Sir, we have no control over McDonald's hours of operation. If we did, then we would be McDonalds."

(We also don't have any control over the taxis. They are free to charge whatever they want. I agree that

209

sometimes it's an outrageous fee. Screaming "How dare you allow them to charge me that much?" is not going to help. What also isn't going to help is taking my name down and trying to report me to the Grand High Wizard of Taxis. I don't work for the cab company.)

"You should. This is called taking care of your guests. Getting me food should be your number one priority. (Sure it is.) You are a hotel, aren't you?"

"Yes, sir, we are a hotel. We are not, however, a fast food restaurant. We do not have the ability to force other businesses to change their hours. That's not the way the world works."

"Dammit! This fucking sucks. I can't believe this bullshit. I hope…"

That's the beauty of customer service. It doesn't matter if I am not offended by your swearing (and let's face it, I could shame sailors with my potty mouth), I still don't have to listen to it. And I can't get in trouble for hanging up in your face. I win again.

But, alas, it doesn't look like that was the last complaint for the night. (Is it ever?)

"I just got back from the game tonight and when I got to my room I found the rollaway bed that I had requested earlier. But it wasn't unfolded for us. You need to do something about that."

Is he serious? Is he really calling to complain because the bed wasn't unfolded for him? Is it going to strain his delicate features to actually push the two sides apart from each other? Should I run up there with the instruction manual or something?

"I'm sorry about that, sir. But all you have to do is open it up and it's all set for you."

"I shouldn't have to open it up myself. You should have to come up here and open it for me. That's called customer service."

Does he want me to hold his hand through this whole ordeal? I really hope that he is going to be able to afford the therapy bills that will result from this trauma. "No, sir. You are more than capable of unfolding the bed on your own."

"I am never staying at this hotel again. The service here is absolutely horrible. If it's not one thing it's another. I honestly don't know how this place has stayed in business."

"Well, sir, the Hilton is just down the road. Feel free to stay there from now on."

The Hilton should really be paying me commission because of how many people go to stay there because of my rudeness. Maybe they will put up with that kind of shit over there (They kind of have to. Look at Paris.), but we don't have to here. We're classier than that. At least we pretend to be.

I get five whole seconds in between phone calls. In that time, I contemplate exactly why I took a job in the hospitality industry when it is so clear that I hate people. What could possibly have made this amount of customer interaction worthwhile? Oh yeah. Complete and utter desperation. Money is a powerful motivator to do things that you despise.

I take a really deep breath to center myself before answering the phone again. I have a feeling that I am going to need all the patience I can get if I am going to make it through this night.

"I just threw up in the hallway outside of my room."

Eww. Am I supposed to be all excited that I'm the first person he called after it happened? "Oookkaaaay." What else can I say to that?

"I expect someone to get up here and clean it before it starts to smell."

Let me get this straight. He threw up in the hallway outside his room. Therefore, it came out of him. And now he has the nerve to call me and be all demanding about it. Really? Where does he get the balls?

I get what the hospitality service entails. I even get the fact that it is our job to go and clean up this man's vomit from the hallway. That is one of the joys of staying in a hotel. You, as the guest, really do not have to do shit. We are here to make your life a little easier. I am okay with the fundamental concept of this. (I know it sounds like I am not, but really I am.) But is it too much to ask for a little courtesy when calling and asking someone to come upstairs to clean up something that came out of your body. I don't think so. Maybe that's just me being a douche.

I have stayed in hotels before. And some of them were just as nice as this one is. I don't ever recall being that big of an asshole to any of the staff. In fact, I always try to be nice to them because, when you think about it, they could do some pretty fucked up shit during your stay. Until I started working here, I never knew exactly how much control hotel workers have over the hotel. It makes me glad that I was always nice. Because I really wouldn't want to have to try to get adult programming taken off my bill. (All the ones that I put on people's bills were eventually taken off, but it was still a pain in the ass to explain that they did not order porn.)

"I will send someone up there to take care of it, sir." I actually feel bad that I am going to have to send someone to do this. No amount of money is worth having to clean up someone's vomit.

"Make sure they get up here soon. I don't want to smell this tonight."

You know what? I think I will call someone in about an hour to clean it up. That should give this asshole enough time to get a good whiff of what he's done. And I hope he

213

doesn't get too comfortable when he climbs into bed because he is most definitely getting a three a.m. wake up call.

I won't lie. Sometimes I am amazed that I haven't gotten fired yet. I'm rude to a lot of people. I am very argumentative with my fellow co-workers, not to mention my boss. And I'm just downright not helpful. To give myself a little bit of credit, I am nice to the ones who are nice to me. (I don't come across a great many of them here, but there are some that are not completely despicable.) I get the feeling that I am living on borrowed time, especially with Doogie watching my back like DCF on Britney's kids.

The Devil Wears An Ugly Pantsuit

A Special Message Concerning the Mating Ritual
of the North American Big Bellied Jackass

Scientists around the world have logged
countless hours studying and trying to understand
the mating ritual of the North American Big Bellied
Jackass. Even though this particular breed is quite
abundant, especially in certain regions of Texas, it
is quite difficult to witness the mating ritual. This is
mainly due to its extremely low success rate.

The Big Bellied Jackass begins the ritual like
most other species, grooming. The most integral
part of the ritual is the Jackass's choice of headgear.
The vast majority of them choose to wear a cowboy
hat when going on the hunt. The hat seems to fill
the Jackass with alarming amounts of confidence
that he should not normally have. Scientists believe
that the hat, in combination with copious amounts
of alcohol, gives the Jackass a false sense of body
type, usually resulting in optical delusions of
decreased belly size and increased penis size. With

mental pictures of what the Jackass believes his body to look like, he proceeds to search for very attractive females who may or may not suffer from some sort of eating disorder. Suffering from delusions, the Jackass feels that these types of women are within his level. Sadly, he is mistaken. His pursuit of these females usually ends in rejection, scorn, and sometimes laughter.

Ultimately, the Jackass comforts himself in more alcohol before returning to his home where the rest of the evening is spent in a frenzy of pornography and masturbation.

Scientists feel that this behavior must be stopped immediately. Not because they are afraid that this ritual will lead to the permanent extinction of the North American Big Bellied Jackass, but simply for the few times that this ritual succeeds. Every time a Jackass has sex, there is a chance of reproduction and that could lead to this behavior continuing in future generations. That is an evolutionary turn that some scientists are not willing to make.

This message has been brought to you by the Partnership for a Stupid Free America. Do your part. Taser a moron!

I would like to know who exactly it was that I pissed off in a past life. I don't see any other reason for the level of torture that I am being forced to put up with. The hospitality industry as a whole, I can tolerate. I will even put up with Doogie to the point where I don't want to punch him in his face. There is just a point where it is time to draw a line in the bullshit. And that point is Leslie.

Leslie is the bitchy sister that no one wants to invite to the family functions because you know she's going to cause some form of a scene over the potato salad being too lumpy, and no one remembers that she hates lumpy potato salad. Then she will run off into the house and drown her sorrows in an economy sized box of wine. This will, of course, lead to her walking around the house in the wedding dress that was being saved for her but never used because all of her boyfriends left her for other men. And then when she finally passes out, the whole family gets together and decides to give her the wrong address next year. She's like that, only worse.

Her last name sounds like something you would hear in an episode of the Golden Girls when Rose goes off into one of her Saint Olaf stories. I won't even being to try to pronounce it. Maybe it's because of her last name that kids made fun of her when she was young so she grew up to be the heinous bitch that she is today. And she really doesn't want to take me on because I will shove some Stroovenhooven right up her ass.

Leslie started working at the hotel about a month ago. She is one of those management interns who just graduated from college with a degree in Hotel Management. (A Word to the Wise: Instead of going to school and getting a useless degree like this, just give someone head. It is more time and cost efficient.) She started off working in the housekeeping department, bossing people around while they folded sheets.

Her career at The Hotel is not going so well. After being kicked out of housekeeping for being a bitch, she was shipped off to reservations. There she lasted an entire week before the head of the department said she refused to work with her. After that, her career as a room service manager lasted two days. (I won't lie. I started hating Lily just a little bit less after that day.) Her next stop was Guest Services but they stopped that before it even started. The head of that department threatened to quit if Leslie was put in her department. And that is how she landed her bony ass at the front desk. (Leeland says it's because they are giving her one last chance, but we all know it's because we are fucking desperate for managers.)

No one is happy about this. We've all heard the horror stories coming from the other departments. I've actually seen her in action. She actually started yelling at one of the housekeepers in the middle of the lobby at four o'clock in the morning on New Year's Day. Then she had the nerve to look at me funny when I told her it might be best if she kept her voice below foghorn level when she is standing in a thirty story lobby. (She shut the hell up though.)

All the front desk agents have gotten together to have our own little meeting and have decided that Leslie is at fault for all the world's problems. (Must be a nice break for Meredith Grey. Don't get too comfortable though, Grey. I'll be back for you.) It's not just that she's a snob and that she's argumentative. It's that she is a real honking bitch when she does it.

Doogie hounds me a lot about professionalism and there are a great many of his suggestions that I truly believe are full of shit, but the one thing I do agree with is that it is not professional to argue with someone in front of a guest. I think this rule should go double for arguing with your employees in front of the guests. But Leslie does not seem to be burdened with this rule. That would explain why she jumped in on my conversation with a guest while I was trying to give him directions to the interstate.

"Oh no. It's much better if you go this way." She begins to draw lines all over the nice map that I just drew for the man. (We were out of the preprinted ones that day.)

I notice that her squiggly lines would take this guy about six miles in the wrong direction to get on the interstate when all he has to do is catch the on ramp two blocks down the road. "No. That's too complicated. There is an on ramp right around..."

"I think I know what I'm doing. Why don't you go and file those registration cards over there?" She turns back to the gentleman that she is trying to get lost in the city. "You want to go seven blocks up this one-way street and turn right. Then you want to go nineteen blocks down this street and take a right. After six blocks you want to take another right."

Is this bitch serious? Does she not realize that she is about to have this man drive in a really huge circle? (Or square?)

"Excuse me. It's pretty obvious that you have no idea what you're talking about, seeing as where he wants to go is only two blocks away. So why don't I help this gentleman while you go over there and be strange?"

"No. I don't..."

"I got this, Leslie. Run along now."

Okay, so maybe that really couldn't be called an argument, but it still shouldn't have happened in front of a guest. Mostly because if she had said one more word I was going to slap the teeth out of her.

Of all Leslie's faults, her biggest one is her appearance. I have nothing against people who like to tan. A good healthy tan can really improve someone's general look. This doesn't apply to me personally, nor does it apply to Leslie. There is a very unnatural orange hue to her skin. It's clear that this woman suffers from a severe case of tanarexia. Someone really needs to take action and conduct some sort of intervention. If I cared enough about the bitch, I would do it myself.

I've been seriously considering trying to save up my money and getting her a really nice green wig. (Real green hair. Not that horse hair weave they sell in the stores.) If she had that then she could possibly have a chance of reclaiming her life as an Oompa Loompa. Then she could spend her days making Wonka bars, frolicking around the chocolate river, and turning selfish girls into blueberries. She also wouldn't have to bitch about all the overtime she has to work. (It's called management, cow. Suck it up.)

Perhaps I shouldn't be so hard on Leslie. I'm sure she's had a very hard life. I mean what with her forced migration from her home in Loompa Land at the hands of the evil Vermicious Knids. But every time I try to pull one ounce of compassion from my hollow shell of a heart, she opens her mouth and reminds me that she is Satan's cold hearted mistress given leave to come to the surface and torture us.

Aden and I are about to go insane. The other managers feel that for Leslie to be completely prepared to work the front desk, she needs to be trained on everything. And that includes the overnight shift. Imagine the joy we are having.

Aden has been trying to explain the night manager reports that she has to work on during the shift and Leslie is just standing there looking confused. I am quite positive that this is not a new look for her. This whole thing is very reminiscent of the whole Autumn debacle. Like me, Aden has a sheet of paper that tells her exactly how to print these reports. And like Autumn, Leslie can't follow what is going on. I really don't understand this because all she has to do is press the numbers that the stupid piece of paper tells her to. People who make things more complicated than they need to be are the devil.

"But what do you do with all these reports once you've printed them?"

"You put in stack and bring to Leeland's desk." The disdain can easily be heard in Aden's voice. I've trained her well, apparently.

I'm watching this whole interaction with a newfound sense of awe. (I may or may not have rushed through my paperwork just so I wouldn't be distracted during this scene.) I just don't understand how someone who made it to management can be so stupid. It is my strong opinion that the majority of people who become managers when they don't deserve it get the job because of sexual favors, but no one can stand Leslie long enough to get a blowjob from her. She has to be related to someone in the company. There is no other way.

I would blame Leslie's confusion on Aden's accent, but I can't. The paper that explains everything is written in perfect English, so this should not be that difficult. I'm beginning to think that she might be just a tad bit slow in the head because if she can't understand the concept of pushing the number four on a keyboard then she's got some serious issues. Maybe that is why she's such a heinous bitch. She's overcompensating for her single digit IQ.

"Hey, Aden. I'm going to run outside and smoke a cigarette. I'll be back in a few." As much as I would like to stay and watch Leslie mess up something that a monkey could be trained to do, it's giving me a headache.

"Can you do that?"

Oh, I just know this bitch is going to be trouble. She couldn't even let me get around the front desk before she had to open her mouth.

"What do you mean? The physical act of smoking a cigarette? I'm pretty sure I can, seeing as how I've been doing it since I was fifteen."

She rolls her eyes at me. There's something else that's going to get her punched in the face. "No. I mean can you just tell her that you're going to have a cigarette? Shouldn't you ask for permission from your manager to take a break?"

Behind Leslie's back I can see Aden trying to hide a smirk. Leslie must be bound and determined to get slapped because she's really asking for it right now.

"Aden and I have an arrangement worked out. As long as all the work is done, she doesn't care if or when I go to smoke a cigarette. Most of the time I try not to leave her when the entire lobby is so full of guests." I sweep my arms out in a grand gesture of sarcasm, pointing out that there is not one single person in the lobby. "But today, I am going to make an exception. Now, when we work together on the overnight shift, which will be never, you are more than welcome to set up some boundaries on my nicotine intake."

Leslie looks pissed and I couldn't be happier about it. There is something about the look on her face when she gets pissed off that brings me joy. Her features twist and turn until she looks like she is about to shit a sixty pound egg. "You never know. They've been talking about putting me on this shift a couple nights a week. We may have to work together more than you think."

"No, we won't. They've already told me that they were thinking about putting you on the shift, and I told them that if they ever scheduled us together that I would call in sick every time. And since I've come to work every day that I've been scheduled, including the day I was in a major car accident, when I had a broken toe, and the day that I had a very serious hangnail, they know it's pretty serious. So you will not be working with me."

In my best impression of a snooty aristocrat, I swing myself around with my nose in the air and leave the front desk. Behind me I can hear Leslie making some muffled complaints and Aden not saying a word. What is she going to do? Report me to Leeland for being mean to her. That won't work for two major reasons. Number 1: This isn't the second grade. Number 2: Leeland can't stand her ass either.

This is all I need right now. Doogie with a vagina.

***

There is a new group coming in and I'm not sure how to handle this. I've been thinking about requesting the entire week off, but Doogie assured me that wasn't going to happen. (Sure I can't get it, but if he needs the week off to bring his girlfriend's big ass to the beach, he gets it.) Something is going to have to be done. And soon.

I pretty much had my fill of children with the church kids whose stink I have finally washed off me. I've already said a million and a half thank you's for my lack of uterus.

225

And I'm so grateful to whatever higher power is out there for making me gay so that children will not factor into my life. Except, of course, at work.

Leslie was giving us the briefing about this group earlier today. She still won't talk to me after our last encounter, so she was addressing everyone else and I just got to overhear it. I made up for it by making weird faces at her throughout the whole meeting. (Who's going to win the award for maturity? So not me.) Philip found it to be very amusing.

The Texas Educational Association of Theaters is the new group that I am going to have to be putting up with for the next five days. (I wonder if they realize that their initials spell TEAT?) I'm sure anyone who is around me can tell just how thrilled I am about this. Because what is the one thing that could possibly be worse than a hotel full of kids? That's right. A hotel full of gay kids. And since I haven't quite entered the 118th circle of hell, let's make them all country bumpkin homos. And since they are in the theater, they have no choice but to be overdramatic. (Like they needed help with that one.)

And this group is coming at the worst possible time. Leslie has decided that she wants to revolutionize the whole front desk department. The first thing she wants to work on is employee morale. My suggestion that she was really not the best person for the job of getting the employees to think nice, happy thoughts was met with a very constipated look. (Why do I get the stern looks for saying what everyone is thinking?)

Our first assignment is to come up with five reasons why we come to work. This is supposed to give us a positive outlook on our job, which will then allow us to be more productive in our work. Then when everyone has done that we are going to post them on a bulletin board in the office. That way we will be able to see what other people's motivation is and be even more motivated. (After we're finished, maybe we can get some construction paper and glitter and make special Valentine's cards for our secret crushes.) Seriously, I haven't been in second grade in a very long time. I do not have any desire to go back.

So that is what I am trying to do right now. It's not very easy to do when I have an entire herd of underage homos running around the lobby. The collective sound of their voices is making dogs seventeen miles away howl. I have attempted to plug my ears with cotton, but Jessie made me take them out. Something about them not being very professional. I smell the influence of Doogie and Leslie.

Honestly, I don't have a problem with homos. (I would be a hypocrite if I did.) It's just that this group is really working my nerves. I do not see the purpose of this little boy strutting through the lobby like he's on a runway with a pink feather boa around his neck and screaming at the top of his lungs, "Don't worry, bitches. Your queen has arrived and she is fabulous." I just don't. Does that actually serve any kind of purpose except to make people think that he should have been born a woman? I am desperately hoping that he is rehearsing for his role in the stage version of Priscilla Queen of the Desert, but I get the feeling that my hopes are for nothing.

And these little divas are so cocky. I've heard three different conversations about how someone thought he totally did the best Madonna at the Superstar Look-a-like Concert (Um… Isn't that just a fancy name for a drag show?) held at the last convention. I can see how these conversations are beneficial to the general population.

"I have an issue with my room. It is not up to my standards at all. Something needs to be done about this."

The kid in front of me cannot possibly be a day over twelve. He's got blonde highlights in his hair and a silver hoop sticking through his ear. How on earth did he convince his parents to let him dress himself this way? (My mother would have FREAKED!)

"What exactly is wrong with it?" What more could this mini Britney in training need to satisfy him/her/it?

"It's just not up to my standards. The bed is not soft enough. The pillows are clearly not genuine goose down. And the sheets are not 1000 thread count like I had requested when we decided to stay here. I am appalled."

I really want to tell Sparky to run along because I've got serious work to do, but I'm afraid I just can't lie that much. Making a ridiculous list of reasons why I come here should not be considered work in any form. But that still doesn't mean that I have time for this preteen diva and his shenanigans.

"Everything in your room is what comes standard in all of our rooms. I'm sure that someone explained that to whoever reserved your stay here. We don't keep 1000 thread count sheets on hand."

"I can't sleep on what you have in that room. I have very sensitive skin and they are just not the quality that I expect."

Is he serious? Am I having some sort of delusion brought on by the smell of the brass cleaner they were using earlier? Maybe, if I try really hard, I will wake up to find this has all been a dream and this kid is not actually in front of me, and Leslie is really off picking Snozberries for the Wonka factory. There has to be some explanation because this diva has not been in any movies, or on a TV show, or released some form of album. I can't understand why he is acting like the second coming of Christina Aguilera.

"Listen up, kid. If you want the accommodations of a luxury resort, then I suggest you go stay at one. Or bring your own sheets for the bed. You can request whatever you

229

want, but we can't give it to you if we don't have it. So until you do either one of those things, you are just going to have to slum it like the rest of the world."

He scoffs at the very idea of having to act like a normal person because in his head he is already a major star. I'll remember that when he's flipping recompressed meat patties at Burger King. (Trust me. My special order will upset him.)

"So, you aren't going to do anything about this?"

"There's nothing I can do. I seem to have lost my ability to pull 1000 thread count sheets from my butt."

"Well I'm not happy."

I'm sure the world is not going to stand for this injustice. So what if there is a war raging on in the world? A poor underage homo is going to have to sleep on regular sheets. It really puts things into perspective, doesn't it?

He storms off. I'm sure he is running right up to his room to comfort himself in his work of rechoreographing the music video to Hit Me Baby One More Time to make it look even sluttier. I'm sad on the inside.

This list is harder than I thought it would be. I imagined myself just writing down the first five things that came to mind, but that didn't exactly work. Then for five seconds I thought about taking it seriously, but I remembered that I can't think of five reasons that I enjoy coming to this place.

It does give me a lot of people to judge, but I don't think that is exactly what Leslie wants. (However true it may be.)

"Excuse me. Where is your hot tub?"

I'm a little taken aback because the question is so polite. It is really sad that this job has made me so accustomed to people being rude that I don't know how to react when some is actually nice. It's along the same lines as what do you do when Paula Abdul isn't acting crazy. It's just not the norm.

"I'm sorry. We don't have a hot tub here. All we have is the pool and it closed at ten o'clock."

"Maaaaaannnn, this suuuuucks." We were doing so well and now he had to go and pull out the whiny voice that sounds like a dying cat's nails on a chalkboard. "I really wanted there to be a hot tub because I wanted to bring my new boyfriend there. We could have a lot of fun. We just met tonight."

Eww. Overshare. I really have no desire to know about the sex life of the average underage homosexual. That's just not on my list of priorities. Besides, aren't these kids too young to know about sex? I thought at their age (which I'm still not too clear on. 12, 14, 5?) they were still worried about cooties and that kind of nonsense. I never once remember as a child being worried about the location of a hot tub so I could do inappropriate things with someone I met five minutes before. (If the children are the future of

231

this country, I am moving to Canada. And this is not a good sign because I hate me some Canada.)

This is hell, isn't it? I have died and gone straight to hell. This is my punishment for being a raging bitch for the vast majority of my life. I have been sentenced to spend eternity with pint sized divas. And if this is hell, then Leslie is clearly Satan's cruise director.

Sean's Five Reasons for Coming to Work

1) To be able to pay for my car
2) To be able to pay for my car insurance
3) To be able to pay for my cell phone
4) To be able to pay for cheese sticks from Sonic
5) Because it gives me an alarming number of people to hate, make fun of, plot the untimely demise of, both co-worker and civilian

(This was only the rough draft of the list. The final draft never made it to the bulletin board because Leeland finally saw it for what it was. Stupid.)

***

Leslie has not been at the front desk for very long, but in her short time here she has managed to secure herself a level of hatred that I had previously only reserved for Doogie. It's a special place where evil thoughts float around about possible bad things that could happen to her. (Ex. Drowning in a large whirlpool of Mrs. Butterworth's syrup. It's threatening and delicious. It's threatlicious!)

But apparently the feeling is mutual. After having a couple days off, I've come back to find that Leslie and Doogie have teamed up together in a cute little co-op of evil. In my opinion, this is stretching the one brain cell that they collectively share past its limit, but no one asked me.

Because Doogie sucks at life, he totally ratted me out that I might have mentioned on my blog that Leslie is an Oompa Loompa from hell. Needless to say, she's not happy about it. (Not that she's ever happy anyway.) Now every time she looks at me, I think she's imagining all the ways she can turn me into a Wonka bar. Not that I really care because my dark thoughts are a lot worse than hers. But she does seem genuinely offended by what I wrote about her, which I do not understand because the bitch knows I hate her. Why so shocked?

Knowing that I had requested certain days off, the Dipshitic Duo put their plan into action. What is their ingenious plan? They have put a filter on all the computers in the hotel so that I can't go to Myspace. Their reasoning?

233

They thought that if they cut off my access to Myspace then I would no longer be able to write horrible things about them.

I didn't think they had enough juice in that poor underused brain cell to come up with a place that is so diabolically evil. If I didn't hate them so much, I might actually be proud. But since I do hate them, I want them destroyed.

They have done like the worst thing ever. I am being sentenced to death by boredom. My job barely takes me forty-five minutes to get done. That leaves me with a lot of time on my hands. You can only play Diner Dash so many times before it gets really old. Myspace has been my salvation. It has given me a public forum in which to spread my bitter ramblings to the public. Not to mention that it has given me quite a few laughs. Especially when I get messages from straight guys who are looking to cheat on their girlfriends so they can have their first man on man experience. (First my ass!)

I just don't get what the big deal is. Myspace is not hurting anyone. Sure, I may have said one or two or twenty bad things about Leslie and Doogie, but it's not like I was using it to troll for nasty skanks. (Yes, the funky valet guy was doing it, but he doesn't work here anymore.) Myspace is good people.

I get their thought process. I do. They think that if they take away Myspace then I will be forced to stop writing such horrible (but true) things about them, therefore causing random people throughout the country to hate them. It is really too bad that their plan has one giant hole in it. What Doogie and his chocolate making cohort don't realize is that I could stop writing completely and people will still hate them. People are still going to say horrible things about Leslie because she is a bitch. And people are going to talk shit about Doogie because when you choose to wear your hair in the shape of a butt, you are kind of asking for it. My comments only add fuel to an already blazing fire.

And, furthermore, I will not be silenced. What Tweedledee and Tweedledumbass don't understand is that I have other ways of accessing Myspace. Like the vast majority of people in the world, I have a computer at home. I can just as easily post my bitter ramblings from there. And also, they forgot to put the filter on one of the computers at the guest services desk, which is a whole twenty feet from where I stand every night. It's a long trek, I know, but if one nasty comment gets posted about Leslie's douchebagesque qualities or Doogie's hair, it will be worth it.

Of course you know, this means war!

Mamas Don't Let Your Babies Grow Up To Be Assholes

An Open Letter to the City of Houston

Dear Someone of Importance in the Government of the City of Houston Who's Name I Do Not Know and Am Far Too Lazy to Google,

As I understand it, The Houston Rodeo has been a tradition for many years, but I don't know exactly for how long. (It is just another one of the reasons that Google makes the world better. But as I've already pointed out, I am too lazy for all that.) It is my opinion, therefore the right opinion, that you should cease having this rodeo immediately.

I'm sure everyone thinks that the rodeo is wonderful because it is such a boost to the economy, but you must think about what it does to the city itself. With this being Texas, I think we already have enough of the cowboy wannabes stuffing their size forty and above bellies into size thirty-two Wranglers. (That in itself is a safety hazard. Only prayer is holding those pants together, and someone will lose an eye when a button pops off.) But when you organize events that are aimed directly at these Southern Rural Folks, you are just asking for them to come to the city.

I do understand the financial aspects of the whole shindig, but what cost are we paying for it? Sure these people bought half a million pounds of Slim Jim's and six hundred thousand cases of chewing tobacco, but is that really worth risking some little girl's eye being poked out by a rogue button for the simple crime of wanting to see Hannah Montana in concert. I think that's too high of a price. Think of the children.

And think of everyone else in the city that does not enjoy cowboy-palooza as much as others. Or the people who are forced to work in the service industry when these people come to town. It is very inconvenient, not to mention annoying when there is a mass influx of these

237

people. There is just not enough Bud Light in the world to make these people happy.

So I beg you to find some other way to supplement the city's income without having this ritual in redneckocity. Start pushing lottery tickets more. Close a couple of schools. Anything. The madness has got to stop. I don't know about you, but if it were me, I wouldn't want any more button related eye injuries on my conscience.

Yours truly,
Sean

I can't think of anything worse to have going on in the city than a rodeo. Maybe I'm just weird, but I don't get it. What is so nice about walking around in the hot sun all day surrounded by livestock? That cannot possibly smell good. Animal poo baked in the sun does not get better over time.

Okay, so there is a Reba McEntire concert in the middle of it all. That's borderline awesome, but I can't get too excited about it because I can't go. Do you know how frustrating it is to be in the same city as one of your favorite people of all time and not be able to go and see them because of some little Oompa Loompa on a power trip? Let's just say that it isn't helping my burning hatred of her.

What also doesn't help matters is that Grace just stopped by the hotel to pick up a copy of this week's schedule and she just got out of the concert. I love Grace to death, but I am hating her just a little bit right now. After Lance Bass coming to sweep me off my feet, my next dream is to be adopted by Reba McEntire. And that's just never going to happen if I have certain people trying to block my dreams, dammit!

But since we, along with every other hotel in the city, are booked to capacity because of this blatant excuse for large men to wear tight blue jeans, I am stuck here. And trust me, this is not nearly the picnic that it sounds like.

For the past two nights the lobby has been filled with people whose main form of entertainment is taped reruns of Hee Haw. This is a group of people who find it acceptable to scream "Yee Haw" as loud as they can at two in the morning. And they also have the nerve to be offended when they are told anything about it. "We're just some good ole country boys trying to have some fun!"

I have nothing against fun. Many people seem to be under the impression that I am some sort of assassin of joy. Yes, sometimes my personality tends to imply that I hate things fun and fun related. I don't. It's just that when someone else's fun impedes on my day, then we have a problem and something must be done about it. Generally that something turns out to be me yelling at someone. And yes, me getting a call from one of the guests saying that someone is trying to use one of the emergency fire hoses to lasso people is something that I would consider impeding on my day.

"Hey! I need some service over here." A rather large specimen of human being slaps his big, beefy hand down on the front desk. I'm sure he thinks that is going to make me more inclined to help him. (It's not.)

I could hurry over there and help him as fast I can, but that would give him the impression that he can just slam his hand down and I'll come running, like this is some sort of country western bar. I firmly believe that it is my responsibility to relieve people of their delusions. They won't know that they are doing something wrong unless I tell them. They obviously can't figure it out for themselves.

"How may I help you, sir?" (Professionalism first!)

"Me and my buddies over there," He points out a large group of men in cowboy hats with unruly mustaches, "are looking for an establishment that features young ladies taking their clothes off." Charming. I guess he thinks if he uses bigger words it won't sound so disgusting. "Can you help us with that?"

What am I? Do I look like the cruise director for Large and Horny Boat Lines? Do I seem like the type of person who has some connection to get these guys into the Grits and Tits down the road? Do I look like some stripper bar aficionado? Is that really the image that I am putting out there? I don't think so, but maybe the alcohol quickly working its way into their bloodstreams has somehow given them a false impression.

"I'm sorry, I really don't know where any of them are."

"Shouldn't you know? You work at a hotel, don't you? Aren't you supposed to know where everything is just in case we want to see some titties?" He punctuates his sentence with a very loud hiccup. I can't imagine why this man couldn't find a woman to come on this trip with him.

"Sir, there are too many bars in this city for me to know the location of them all. I am not required to know where

241

they are. You might want to look on the internet to see if you can find anything. I'm sure there is an entire section where you can look for "titty bars"." I sort of have to hate myself a little bit for actually doing the finger quotes.

"You must not like titties. Is that it?"

"My like or dislike of breasts is not the issue here, sir."

"Just admit you don't like titties."

Why do I suddenly feel like I'm back in kindergarten and the school bully is trying to make me admit that I have cooties? I get the fact that this guy probably doesn't have anything above a first grade education but I would think he'd have grown up a little over the years.

Now I'm contemplating sending him and his little posse over to the only gay bar I know. And because I really don't like these people, that's exactly what I do. (I'm already going to hell, I might as well have a little fun on the way.) I can only imagine what their faces are going to look like when they see a bunch of tweaked out boys all over each other instead of their much sought after "titties". I guess I should be ashamed of myself, but I'm not, so why should I pretend?

I think it has been well catalogued about my hatred for people who use the word titties. I have no sympathy. And while I doubt it, I hope some little homo high on crystal meth tries to grab that man's ass.

***

One of the good things about working the overnight shift, even with all the crazy people, is that generally it's just me and the supervisor working. That is unless it is really busy and Doogie or Leslie is staying late to help out. (In which case, hell may be freezing over because those bitches hate working extra hours.) Because it's usually just me with Aden or Jessie, we tend to goof off a lot. One of our pastimes is making prank phone calls to Doogie. (Our little hoochie text messages are a thing of the past. We have moved on to bigger and better things.)

Jessie and I have been taking turns being a hooker and a pimp. She really has the part down and I have a surprisingly good "Bitch, where my money?" What makes this even better is knowing that I am actually getting paid to harass my boss right now.

Doogie's fiancé didn't care too much for those text messages we sent. Let's just say that she enjoys these prank phone calls even less. Her voice tends to go up a couple of octaves when she is screaming from across the room. "Why hookers be calling this late at night? How they get your number?" I take some satisfaction in knowing that Doogie is not getting any tonight. (This is exactly why I've never given them my cell phone number.) It's things like this that make me laugh myself into an asthma attack at the front desk.

My abrupt laughing fit is put on hold because of the sound of a blood curdling scream coming from the front doors. This is not the kind of scream that you might hear every day. Or the kind that might come from your mouth when Meredith Grey is doing something extremely slutty. This is a horror movie, some blonde girl in high heels is getting stabbed in her boobs kind of scream.

I freeze because I obviously think someone is currently dying in the lobby, and I have no idea what to do. Do I check it out first? Or do I call 911 first and ask questions later? Maybe I should boil some water for some reason. (Clearly, I am absolutely useless in an emergency.) Jessie starts snapping into action while I stand here like a mannequin displaying this year's poo brown fashion. If I'm ever dying in a hotel, I want Jessie to be around.

I see a man running through the lobby towards the front desk. He is carrying a woman over his shoulder. She's the one screaming her lungs out. This I really don't understand. Is he kidnapping her? If he is, then he is quite possibly the stupidest kidnapper ever. I don't think the first rule of abduction is to bring her to a very public hotel lobby filled with people who can hear her screams. To me, that just seems to be the complete opposite of what you would want to do. But what do I know, I've never kidnapped anyone before. (Just because I sometimes plan Doogie's kidnapping when I'm drifting off to sleep doesn't mean that I have had practice.)

As they get closer I can see that this guy is clearly in town for the rodeo. Between the ripped blue jeans and the long, glorious mullet, there's no mistaking it. And the screaming woman looks like she just got off a double shift at the Waffle House with her too much make up and her bouffant hair knocking on Heaven's door. There are dark lines of mascara running down her face from her tears.

Country Bumpkin Kidnapper comes up to me and drops Waffle House Lady right on the desk. Usually this a great big no-no because I thoroughly despise spending my night wiping ass prints off the faux marble, but I'm letting this slide because this woman is apparently in some kind of great physical pain.

"Is she okay? Is there anything I can do to help?" (See now. Not so evil inside all the time.)

"We just walked all the way from the rodeo and her feet are killing her. She just couldn't do it anymore."

I know that, deep down in my soul, I just hallucinated. There is no possible way that this woman came in here making a scene and is now sitting on my desk because her feet hurt. I am going to have to spend valuable time that could be otherwise used productively (Not really, but he doesn't have to know that.) cleaning the marks that her ass is permanently imbedding on my front desk because she tried to shove her big clown feet into some hooker heels and decided to walk seventeen miles. NO SHE DIDN'T!!!!! (I'm wondering if anyone will ever be able to document the exact second that I transform into a strong, black woman.)

"Get her off my desk! What are you? Crazy?"

"But, man, her feet are killing her. Can't you see that she is in pain here?"

"Then make her take off those fourteen inch heels and maybe her feet won't hurt so badly." Did they seriously not know that that was the cause of her problem?

"OH MY GOD!!! It hurts. I need a wheelchair. I can't walk anymore." What's more amazing to me is that she is actually able to pick up her head. Judging from the size of her hair, I would have thought that her neck would have snapped by now.

"I am not giving you a wheelchair, ma'am. We only have a certain number of them and they are for our guests with real disabilities." (As much as I would like it to be, stupidity is not, nor will it ever be, classified as a disability.)

"But I can't walk. I can't. I just can't."

My feet hurt too. I have been standing up all night behind this front desk in fucking ugly shoes, but you don't see me bitching about it. Okay, so yeah I am bitching about it, but at least I am not screaming bloody murder.

Before Waffle House Lady can plead anymore about her aching feet and my heartless attitude towards them, I see Jessie coming around the desk pushing a wheelchair. If only Santa had given me the power to shoot death rays from my eyes like I asked when I was a child I could reduce Jessie to a mere pile of ashes. But no. I was never given that ability. (Thanks for nothing, Santa!)

"Oh, thank you. Thank you. Thank you."

Country Bumpkin Kidnapper shoots me an evil look as he deposits Waffle House Lady into the wheelchair and starts pushing her away. As they are moving farther way and out of range of my imaginary death rays, I can see that Waffle House Lady's neck is losing the battle against her hair.

"Why did you do that?" I pull out a cloth and industrial size can of Pledge and start the monumental task of getting her ass marks off my desk. "That bitch didn't need a wheelchair. She could have walked. She just didn't want to." (And if I can't get a wheelchair for that reason, no one should be able to.)

"Sean, sometimes it is just easier to give the stupid people what they want instead of arguing with them. It got rid of them a lot quicker than you trying to make them see how stupid they were being."

I'm well aware that she has a very valid point. But I felt like arguing. I felt that those two stupid people should be held accountable for their decision to act like complete retards. Besides the longer that it took them to see the error of their ways, the longer that they would be inconvenienced. And there is nothing I love more in the world than inconveniencing the guests. Since they so clearly get the same joy out of doing it to me.

I spend the next few minutes hating on Jessie and trying to use my mental powers to influence events so that Waffle House Lady will choke on a waffle when she gets back to work. But, as all things, that cannot last because of the phone.

"Front desk. This is Sean. How may I assist you?" I swear one day I am going to find the person responsible for making me say that phrase and destroy them.

"I need help! It's an emergency!"

I would take this call seriously if it weren't for the fact that I can clearly recognize Waffle House Lady's voice. That and the echo coming from the twelfth floor is a complete giveaway.

"Yes, ma'am, I'm sure it is." If she tells me that her big emergency is that she broke a fingernail, I am going to go throw her off the railing.

"I can't remember my room number."

"Are you serious? That is in no way classified as an emergency. What are you smoking? Seriously."

"I can't remember my room number. I'm scared." This woman's melodrama is off the charts. I thought that life saved this kind of overdramatic performance for junior high school plays.

"You are in room 1225. Please don't call me back unless you have an actual emergency."

I slam the phone down to get out some of my rage. It doesn't work of course because I have entirely too much rage inside of me to be suppressed by the simple act of slamming the phone. It would require more drastic measures like setting Doogie's desk on fire. That's a good one. I will have to add that to the list.

"Did that bitch actually forget her room number?" I am blaming Jessie for inflicting Waffle House Lady on me. If I had been able to argue with her more then she would have been far too scared to call the front desk for such ridiculousness. Though, if that were the case I am sure we would find her in the morning huddled up in the hallway using her hooker heels as a pillow.

"Yes, she did. Now do you see what happens when you pander to the stupid people? They think they can get away with shit like this."

The phone rings again and the caller ID shows that it is room 1225. I'm sure that this will be fun.

"What?" Doogie might say that my greeting is unprofessional, but I call it necessary.

"Oh my god! It's an emergency!"

"What now?"

"We just got back to the room and saw that we have to have our breakfast orders for room service in by eleven. We missed it and we need to order breakfast."

The noise that fills my head is the sound of my last nerve being gotten on. "We obviously have two very different definitions of the word emergency. You are not having an emergency at the moment."

"But what are we going to do? We need to order breakfast."

I take a few calming breaths. Before I start yelling at Waffle House Lady, I decide to take a different approach. Maybe if I try Jessie's approach these people will leave me the fuck alone. "Okay. Here's what I will do. If you promise to go to bed right now and to lose the number to the front desk for the rest of the night, I will go pick up your breakfast order. Just leave it on the door." It's physically painful to compromise with this woman.

"Okay. I'll do that right now."

I want to tell her that if she calls the front desk again, that I will consider that breaking our verbal contract and I will personally insure that her breakfast ends up in any orifice other than her mouth, but I keep my mouth shut in hopes that the interaction between us will be over now.

"Watch the front desk, Jessie, I have to go pick up Waffle House Lady's breakfast order. Unless you want that honor."

"Oh no. I wouldn't want to deprive you."

I throw a crumpled up piece of paper at her. "Just so you know, when we are in hell, I am so not sharing my rock with you."

Up on the twelfth floor, I take a moment to enjoy the quiet. On nights like this there are not many moments where there is complete silence. With the phone ringing and people bitching all the time, one could easily lose his mind. Up here, I can have a few blissful seconds to pretend that it is not my job to help these people.

I grab the breakfast order that almost became a 911 call. Because I can't resist, I have to see what these two brain surgeons ordered for breakfast. They just don't strike me as Sticky Bun French Toast people to me.

The breakfast menu is simple. It lists off everything that the kitchen serves and all the guests have to do is check off what they want to order. It really only takes the most basic skill to master. Pre-schoolers throughout the country don't seem to have a problem with it anyway. So I can't figure out why they decided to write two BLT sandwiches at the bottom of the menu. And it's not even one of the things listed.

I pause for a moment. Sure it would be really simple for the kitchen to throw together two BLT sandwiches and slap them on a plate for these two. But if I let this slide, not only will I have to deal with the morning shift supervisor, Carol, (who is just as evil as Lily only with better hair) for letting people order off the menu, but these people will continue to think that they can do shit like this whenever and wherever they please.

I take out my Pen of Judgment which I keep handy for just such an occasion. I never know when I might need it to make fun of someone. (I don't think this is what the Boy Scouts had in mind when they said "Be Prepared".)

In my best handwriting I write, 'The kitchen can only take orders that are actually on the menu. Handwritten substitutions are not acceptable. Please feel free to order something ON THE MENU in the morning.' I thought this was a more acceptable solution than actually filling out the order with the most expensive things on the menu for them.

After I slide the menu back under the door I walk away with a sense of accomplishment. I have made it possible for these two people to learn that they are idiots and now they can do something about it. They have been armed with knowledge. Maybe I have saved some other poor unsuspecting retail or hospitality worker from having to deal with that bullshit. I should win some kind of award for all the humanitarian work I do. (Move over Tyra. I am so the new Oprah.)

***

I am so over this rodeo. I came into work tonight to find that Country Bumpkin Kidnapper and Waffle House Lady actually had the nerve to request a refund because the kitchen would not make them BLT sandwiches. Apparently my attempts to destupidify them were all for nothing. Maybe I shouldn't be expecting that Nobel Peace Prize anytime soon.

You Are Not Special

A Letter To A Bunch Of People Who Think They Are More Important Than They Actually Are

Dear Silver Club Members,

I thought I should write to you to let you know that none of you are in any way special. I know that you are under the false impression that you are because of the way every single one of you act when you come in here. You should probably realize now that I am not going to get on my knees and kiss your ass for the simple fact that you walked through the door. Because, quite frankly, I don't know where your ass has been.

I'm well aware of the fact that you spend a lot of money at our chain of hotels, but that really does not give you the right to act like a total douchebag. And I know that they gave you one of those little black cards that you think is a license to jackassdom, but it is really not. You are just like the rest of the people in the world.

You do not get a free pass to treat people like garbage just because you deem them unimportant. And really, that's kind of the same way that I see you.

Because I'm nice, I am going to let you in on a little secret. That little black card that all of you wave around as a sign of your superiority? All that really gets you is a complimentary plate of stale crackers and hard cheese. Not really the lifestyle that you envisioned, is it? I hate to be the one to shatter your rosy glasses, but someone had to do it.

And just so you know, I'm a member of the Priority Club at Holiday Inn and I get a lot better service than you ever would here just by not being a donkey. You might just want to take a moment to think about that.

Sincerely,

Sean

Grace, Doogie, and I are sitting in the back. Just like every other time that the three of us are stuck in the back together, I am trying to contain myself from ripping off Doogie's head and using it as a volleyball. (Really the only thing keeping me from doing it at this point is that I really suck at volleyball.) Grace is sitting in the corner trying to contain herself so that she doesn't laugh at my blatant disregard for Doogie's authority.

"I honestly just cannot force myself to care about this issue."

"Sean, it's your job to care. This is your place of employment"

Normally, I would almost agree with him. If the issue at hand were maybe doing something about the crappy computer system or getting some money together to ship Leslie to the moon, I would be the first to be throwing out ideas. I just don't have an opinion on changing our uniforms from poo brown to vomit green. These are not exactly the hot button issues that I give a shit about.

"Right now, you have us dressed like UPS just threw up all over us. Now you want to make it look like someone actually did throw up on us. Either way, we just got puked on. So what does it really matter?"

I can see the wheels in Doogie's head turning to try to come up with some argument for that. He's failing miserably.

We all shut up when the door opens and Leeland steps in. I don't think any of us are quite stupid enough to have this conversation when he is in earshot. I might enjoy a good fight with Doogie but I'm not willing to let Leeland see me openly antagonizing him. Because if he did, then he would know that Doogie has been right all this time. And that is just unacceptable.

"Okay, people, this month we have a lot of Silver Club Members staying with us. We have to make sure we are prepared. Doogie, can you tell me the proper procedure for checking in a Silver Club guest."

This is one of those priceless moments in life that you just wish you had a camera so you could record and enjoy it over and over again. Doogie has very nearly shit his pants. He squirms in his chair because he obviously doesn't know the answer. It's times like these that I believe that life loves me.

"What about you, Sean? Since Doogie obviously doesn't know the answer, can you tell me the correct procedure?"

This is unexpected. While I was spending time enjoying the fact that Doogie was squirming, I completely forgot that I don't know the answer either. In my defense, I am not a manager so I shouldn't have to know these answers. That is merely one of the perks of being the lowly Night Auditor.

But since I can't leave Leeland hanging, I guess. "Just like any other VIP except with more sucking up."

"Essentially, yes."

Wow. That was kind of a shock. Who knew that my smartass mouth would give me the right answer? I am going to take a little joy out of that. Meanwhile, Doogie is across the room about to melt into his seat from anger. This much joy should be illegal.

"You know, Sean, I think you are going to make a fine manager someday."

Laughing in Leeland's face is probably not the wisest course of action right now. Namely because he is clearly on some form of illegal substance and people can be very unpredictable when they are high. And if it's not drugs, then it is some form of mental psychosis. Either way, laughing could get me killed.

I am rude. Confrontational. Arrogant. And sometimes just downright mean. I am not sure these are the qualities that one looks for in a manager. I mean, yes, Doogie is many of these things, but he is not the example I look up to when trying to describe a good manager. A punk ass bitch who needs a new haircut. Sure, I'll look to Doogie for that.

Clearly, Leeland has to be thinking of someone else when he is making this manager comment. He cannot possibly be talking about me.

And then I see the look on Doogie's face. His reaction to Leeland's comment is absolutely beautiful. It is a perfect mixture of rage, hurt, and utter disbelief. And it hits me. Maybe Leeland doesn't mean that at all. Unless he is suffering from some sort of mental disorder, how could he? But what if he just said it to fuck with Doogie? What if he gets the same cheap thrill out of harassing him that I do? I do a quick scan of his face to see if there are any signs that I might be right, but there is nothing.

Might as well go with it then. "I look forward to the opportunity to prove you right someday."

While Doogie sits there fuming, I gather my deposit together. I am curious to see if he is so pissed off that I could fry an egg on his head. But really that's just an excuse for me to throw an egg at him.

I get up to run out the office just as Leeland is about to leave. I don't want to be stuck in that office without Leeland's protection right now. I follow him out, but me being me, I couldn't leave it alone. I turn around to look at Doogie and stick out my tongue. (Yes, I am already writing my acceptance speech for the maturity award.)

When we get out of the office, I start to move in the opposite direction because I am parked on the street.

"Just so you know, I saw that."

Leeland starts going toward the elevators. It might be just my imagination, but I swear I see a smile working its way across his face.

***

"I swear, if Ms. Brock calls one more time, I am going to shove her phone up her ass."

"What bitch want now?" Aden is just as fed up with this woman as I am. And she has every right to be. This woman checked in fifteen minutes ago and has already called to complain three times. I'm sorry if her bed is not facing in the direction that she likes, but I just don't care.

"She wanted to complain that her room is not on one of the higher floors. Like it really matters. Even if you go to one of the higher floors, the view is still of the building next door." (I once had a complaint because a woman looked out her window and saw a couple having sex in one of the offices. What exactly am I supposed to do about that? Like I have control over other people's carnal intentions.)

"We tell her that it is only room. Why she no understand?"

I refuse to believe that Aden's broken English had anything to do with it and that it is all the fault of Ms. Brock's inability to understand the simplest of concepts.

"Because she is evil, Aden. Her sole mission in life is to make our lives miserable."

As if to prove my point, the phone rings. I don't even have to look at the caller ID to know that it is Ms. Brock. I pull myself together enough to get the standard front desk greeting out and not snap at her like I am dying to do.

"There's no ashtray in this room."

"That's because that is a non-smoking room, Ms. Brock."

"Well then why am I in here? I specifically requested a smoking room."

Think happy thoughts. Think happy thoughts. Puppies. Christmas presents. Doogie getting run over by a stampeding elephant. "Yes, ma'am, but like we explained to you earlier, the hotel is full tonight and there were no smoking rooms available when you arrived."

"You know I am a Silver Club member, right? Why wasn't one held for me? I spend a lot of money in this place and I would think that my request isn't that difficult."

"According to our records, you made your reservation two hours before you arrived. Most of these reservations were made well in advance. Since they had already checked in before you made your reservation, we were not able to hold a room for you."

"I don't understand why you couldn't have done it?"

Seriously? Even though I just finished explaining it to her? She still doesn't get it? Now we are not only responsible for pleasing the guest every second of every day, but now we have to be able to tell the future too? Does she truly believe that we employ a bank of psychics to tell us when a Silver Club member might be thinking about making a reservation so we can plan appropriately? (I'm sure Ms. Cleo could use the work. Call me now!)

"Because, like I just explained to you, all of the rooms were already gone at the time you made your reservations."

"Well, I am smoking in this room, so I need an ashtray."

"I'm sorry, Ms. Brock, but you can't smoke in the room. As you can see on the desk, there is a sign that says that smoking in a non-smoking room will result in a $250 deep cleaning charge." (This is such bullshit. I smoke in the non-smoking rooms all the time and never once has anyone told me anything about it. They can't even tell.)

"You will most certainly be waiving that charge for me tonight. It's not my fault that you did not hold a smoking room for me when I so clearly requested one."

"Ms. Brock," I am trying my best to keep my cool, but she is not making it easy, "the smoking fee cannot be waived, even for Silver Club members." I added that last part because I just know she is going to bring it up again. "That is coming from the general manager of the hotel. There is nothing I can do about it. In fact, it's already been added since I can hear you taking a drag on a cigarette."

"Do you have any idea how much money I spend here?" I know of at least $250 dollars. "I think I deserve better treatment than this." Of course you do, honey. Shall I get on my knees and begin kissing your shoes now?

This conversation right here reminds me of why I started the phrase, "Brock rhymes with cock," flying around the front desk. This woman is the perfect example of why I hate all the Silver Club members. She honestly believes that she should be treated better than everyone else just for the simple fact that she is her. That's not really going to happen, and she would be a lot better off as soon as she realizes it. I may be pleasant to her because they pay me to, but take away that paycheck and bitch better watch herself.

"I will pass your comments on to the front desk manager, but at this time that is all I can really do." I really hope she doesn't expect me to pull another smoking room out of my ass for her. That's just not physically possible.

"No, I expect you do something right this..."

"Have a good night, Ms. Brock." I hang up the phone before she can say another word because, if she does, she is never going to shut up.

I make a quick call to the hotel operator, Stella, asking her to disconnect Ms. Brock's phone until six in the morning. Technically, I am only allowed to do this when a guest starts cursing me out, but I am willing to take the punishment if I don't have to hear the sound of Ms. Brock's voice for the rest of the night. Besides, Stella will do it for me anyway. She owes me after not spreading it around the whole hotel that she set her weave on fire with a cigarette. (I only spread it over the internet.)

It's times like this that I wish we could charge the Silver Club members extra just for being assholes instead of giving them a discount for it. If I ran this hotel, things would be different. That's just another thing that I have to work on when I marry Lance Bass and buy this place.

***

Leslie is getting on my nerves. Not that this is a new occurrence with her, but it's really bugging me right now. I really wish I had the authority to send her on some errand that would cause her to get lost in the bowels of the hotel only to be found years later, having reverted to an animalistic state and feeding on rats. But I don't have that kind of power. (And for that Leslie had better be thankful.)

"Why aren't these amenity cards in alphabetical order?" Her voice makes me want to punch her in the face. It would almost be worth going to jail for it.

"Why would they be in alphabetical order? They go by order of their room number." The Hotel is trying out a new special service for our Silver Club members. To give them an even bigger false impression that they are special, we have decided to give them a choice of what amenity they would like in their room. Their choices are the stale cheese and crackers, a plate of crappy bagels, or a really cheap bottle of wine. So far, they have not been enthused. (I'm crying on the inside, I swear.)

"No, they are supposed to go in alphabetical order."

There was a memo on this and everything. Apparently one of Leslie's skills is not reading. Why are we even arguing about this? Why is she even in my space?

"Room service requested that they be put in order by room number so that they can go floor by floor." Obviously Leslie doesn't check her e-mail or she would already know this. It's also apparent that she doesn't check her e-mail or she would see the vast amounts of lesbian porn I signed her up for.

"That doesn't make any sense. You should put them in alphabetical order anyway."

I cannot hit my boss. I cannot hit my boss. I cannot hit my boss. I have a feeling my mantra is about to stop working. "What doesn't make sense is that you are arguing about this when you obviously know nothing about it. Would you like me go get the memo that proves you wrong?" I kept it just in case this very conversation arose.

"I think it makes much better sense to do it my way. I am going to talk to Leeland and tell him that he needs to change it."

I close my eyes and take some calming breaths. My meditative thoughts of puppies and Doogie's demise are not really helping me at all. I need something stronger to block out the annoyance factor of Leslie. Hell, I might even need some chemical assistance. Her persistence to be aggravating is a force to be reckoned with.

"What are you doing?"

Besides hating on her? "I'm trying to find my happy place so I don't go mental patient all over you."

The look on her face is a mix of shock and anger. It's probably the same look she had when she realized that she had escaped the horrors of Loompa Land just to get stuck working in the Wonka factory. "You do realize that I am your manager?"

"If that's what you want to call it. Basically all you do is whine about how unfair everything is for you. Those are not the best qualities in a manager."

266

Leslie looks like I just slapped her in the face. Which I guess I kind of did. I'm not quite sure how she manages to fool herself, but I think she honestly believes that she is the best thing to ever happen to the management profession. Clearly, she is just as delusional as some of our guests.

"You need to start showing me the respect I deserve, Sean. Your attitude is completely unprofessional."

Granted, she is right, but she has obviously never looked in a mirror before. "My attitude? Have you ever had yours checked? You are openly confrontational with other employees in front of the guests. You tell the guests that we don't know what we are talking about. You are rude to everyone you work with. You make it absolutely impossible not to hate you."

The look on Leslie's face is nothing but pure shock. She looks unbelieving that someone would actually speak to her this way, which I think is a major load. I cannot be the first person to ever say these things to her. Someone in her past had to have had enough with her. Her family. Former coworkers. The man she tricked into marrying her by pretending to be a decent human being.

"You know I could give you a write up for talking to me like that."

"A write up for what? Telling the truth? Face it, Leslie, your attitude stinks. No one in this hotel can stand you. And it's all because of the way you treat people. No one is going to give you the respect that you think you "deserve" (Oh yeah. I busted up the air quotes on that one) when you act the way you do. Just because they slapped a title in front of your name does not automatically get you respect. Why don't you try respecting some of the people you are so busy bossing around like a bully and you might earn some back?" (This is so after school special I could vomit.)

"Well, I am the boss. It's my job to tell people what to do."

"No, it is your job to supervise us in our jobs, not to order us around like your own personal servants."

This is the point where she decides to get huffy. "I most certainly do not order people around."

"Okay, so apparently I was the only one around on New Year's when you started screaming in a thirty story lobby because one of the housekeepers didn't pick up a scrap of paper that you told her to. I guess I just hallucinated that."

"That was a completely different situation." She crosses her arms over her chest and sticks her bottom lip out like a petulant child.

"Leslie, you have a lot more in common with our guests than I think you would like to admit, especially our Silver Club members. It's always 'I want this' and 'I want that' and you think a well-placed temper tantrum will get you whatever you want. It doesn't always work out that way."

268

I can see in her eyes that she is thinking about what I have said to her. It must be really taxing for her half of a brain cell. In spite of everything, I hope she actually listens to what I say. It would make me feel good to bring someone back from the evil wasteland where I am sure her soul resides. We could be well on our way to a Hallmark moment here.

"I think I am going to have a talk with Leeland about your attitude."

So close to actually learning something. Yet, too stupid to actually grasp anything. If she's not going to try, then neither am I.

"Leeland doesn't like you either."

The next night, I come in to find a note from Leeland waiting for me:

> *While you may be right, please bring any problems you have with Leslie to me.*

Bitch still didn't get me written up.

***

It's six a.m. and all I can think about is my bed. It's been a very long night and I am counting the minutes until it is over. Aden is standing next to me at the desk and we are nothing but a couple of zombies. We have spent the whole night running around this hotel, and now that people have finally begun to shut up, it is time for morning wake up calls. This is the kind of day that can only be fixed with some sort of sleeping pill, so I can pretend that it never happened. If only it would just end.

The phone rings and I swear Aden actually growls at it. Seeing that it is just Stella and not a guest calling, I quickly pick it up.

"The dumbass in 3031 won't answer his phone for his wake up call. Aden needs to go wake him up."

I get that we are a hotel and our main priority is service, but I think that is going to an extreme. If the guy sets a wake up call and can't wake up for it, I don't see how that is our problem. Are we really expected to go into his room and gently nudge him until he wakes up? How about we give him a gentle kiss on the forehead to rouse him from dreamland while we're at it?

In reality I am well aware of the fact that I making too big a deal out of this. But I have had a very long night, and I feel like being a bitch. Since I actually like Aden, I can't take it out on her, so that only leaves the guests to suffer my wrath. Like the ranting I do in my head can really be considered wrath.

I look at Aden and already know that I am going to be one doing this wake up call. Last time I checked I worked in a hotel not a day care center. This should, in no way, be my job.

"Just give me the master key and I will save you the time of begging me to do it."

Now this may seem extremely pussy of me, but I am making the security guard, Deputy Donothing, come with me. Let's face it, I have no idea what is going on in that room. There might be an ax murderer waiting in that room to prey on poor innocent front desk workers. This could be a scam that he has pulled throughout the country. And I really don't want my skin to be used in the making of any kind of garment. I realize the likelihood of that happening is slim, but all the same, unless there are kids in that room that I can scare the crap out of, I'm not going in alone.

The elevator ride to the thirtieth floor is rather unpleasant. Deputy Donothing does not particularly care for me and I have never made it a secret that I despise him and everything he stands for. Clearly, we aren't speaking to each other. He is resenting me for actually making him do something. And I am resenting him for making more money than I do.

When the elevator doors open I can immediately tell something is wrong, though I am not sure exactly what it is. My spidey sense is tingling. Carefully I step out into the hallway, guarding myself should any supervillains try to attack. That's when I step in it.

271

The squish that my foot makes stepping on the carpet tells me that the carpet is soaked. I don't even have to look at how the carpet is a shade darker over here in the wet while farther down the hall it is the same dry color it's always been, but I do anyway, just to piss myself off more.

Like I even have to ask where the water is coming from. It is no doubt coming from 3031. Where else would it be coming from? This is me we're talking about here. There is no chance that it could be coming from anywhere other than the room that I am on my way to. I can already see the veritable swamp forming right outside the door.

I can feel the water getting into my shoes as I pound on the door. There is nothing in the world that I hate more than getting water in my shoes. It makes my feet all gross and only adds to my general grumpy demeanor. Whoever is in this room should be very afraid. And I take that because he isn't answering the door, he is.

Using the trusty master key that has given me so much joy in the past, I enter the very bowels of hell.

The inside of the room is hot and muggy. It reminds me of my childhood days in Louisiana when I would laugh at my mother because she would actually expect me to leave the air conditioning to go outside and play in weather like this. I didn't find it amusing then, and I most certainly do not find it amusing now. Especially with the feeling of water rushing between my toes with each step I take.

The thing about 3031 is that it is one of our master suites. It is fucking huge. I have lived in apartments that could fit into here. People pay small fortunes to spend one night in this room. And I can pretty much tell from where I am standing, in the entrance, the whole room is soaking wet and completely ruined.

I can hear the shower running in the bathroom, but I don't need that to tell me where the water is coming from because there is a river flowing out of the door. Going against my very nature, I snap into action.

No longer caring about the water and the effect that it is having on my feet, I run into the bathroom where the bathtub is overflowing. It takes me about half a second to find the problem. There is a towel shoved into the drain. Not covering it. Shoved in there on purpose. Someone is going to pay for this. Turning off the shower and removing the towel, the water starts draining quickly. I take a deep breath, grateful that it was a simple problem and not some major plumbing malfunction that I couldn't do anything about. That breath turns out to be a very bad idea.

The smell hits me like a bitchslap across the face. It is straight up public toilet. I am really scared of why that is. Turning around, I see it. Shit. Literally. All over the place.

It is covering the toilet, the sink, and the walls. It looks like someone's ass exploded in here. I have to fight my first instinct, which is to projectile vomit.

I run out of the bathroom before I add to the mess that is already stinking up the tiny room. The sight that awaits me in the rest of the room doesn't do anything to ease my stomach. Staring right at me from the middle of the bed is a really ugly bare ass. It almost sends my stomach over the edge. At this point, I am seriously considering just getting it over with. The room is already fucked, how much damage could a little vomit do?

Mr. Bareass has not moved an inch since I came in this room, which is saying something, because I'm not exactly trying to be quiet. I give myself a minute to calm down so I don't walk over to the bed and beat this guy with a pillow until he wakes up. That would be bad, even if it is completely called for.

Meanwhile, Deputy Donothing is just standing in the doorway doing what he does best. Nothing. If this is what he does during his shifts as a real cop, I am not at all enthused about the response I will receive should I ever get mugged.

With my fist clenched so tight that my knuckles are white, I stand at the edge of Mr. Bareass's bed. I don't want to open my mouth in fear that I might say something that would get me in trouble with the bosses, especially seeing as I am not supposed to be in here right now. The last thing I need is to get Aden in trouble with me. I try to take one last deep breath without taking in any of the smell before I speak.

"GET THE FUCK UP!"

I really might want to reconsider my calming techniques because they don't seem to be working so well.

Mr. Bareass jumps at my scream and flips over giving me a view of something that I could have lived my entire life without seeing. "What the fuck?"

"That's what I was going to ask you. What is going on in here?"

He tries to look around but I can tell he's having trouble seeing. From the smell of him, he has to be hung over to a massive degree. As if the shit smell wasn't enough. "I don't know."

"Sir, please put some clothes on." I am really tired of trying to avert my eyes from the grossness he has going on down there. And it is really hard to direct my rage at him when I have to look at the window.

He stumbles around looking for some clothes to put on. "Hey, the floor's all wet."

"Yes, that tends to happen when you leave the shower running and put a towel in the drain."

"I didn't do that."

"Oh ok. Then it must be one of the little goblins that we have running around the hotel who break into rooms and clog the bathtubs up. That's been a real problem lately."

He is obviously too hung over or possibly still too drunk to process my sarcasm. "My stuff better not be ruined."

"Our room better not be ruined. This room is a little more expensive than your stuff."

He pulls on a pair of shorts to cover himself, but the damage to my retinas is already done. And I would like to get out of here before my olfactory senses start to disintegrate.

"Okay, you have like five minutes to get downstairs to the front desk, so we can figure out what to do about this. I will get maintenance up here and try to salvage something from this mess. But we can't continue this conversation up here because I can't breathe this air for another minute without throwing up all over you."

Not even waiting for a response (because what could he say at this moment that would make this any better) I storm out of the room. What pisses me off is that I don't even get a good storm out scene because of the damn squishing my stomping is making. There is nothing more important to a gay man than making a dramatic exit and squishy shoes do not fit into that scene.

The ride back down to the lobby does nothing to calm me down. Mostly because I have to ride with Deputy Donothing and I want to direct my rage at him, but can't because he has a taser and a gun. And what makes it worse is that he finds this extremely funny. There is nothing funny about a man turning one of our suites into a frat house after Hell Night. (In hindsight, a little funny.)

My shoes are still squishing when I get back to the front desk. Aden, just looking at me, takes a step back. "What fuck?"

Pulling up the room in the computer, I see something that doesn't surprise me at all. "Of course he's a fucking Silver Club member."

"What happen?"

"He shit. Literally shit all over the place." When talking about shit, I should probably lower my voice, but I can't help it. "The walls and the sink and the floor are covered in shit."

"No, he not do that."

"Yes he did. And he completely flooded the room. You need to call maintenance because the room is completely ruined. And so is the hallway."

While Aden makes the phone calls, I try to calm myself down. Never having been hit in the face with the smell of shit everywhere, I have no reference as to how to calm myself. I don't think I have any Doogie demise

277

scenarios that are powerful enough for this. I mean if I combine a couple of them, then maybe. I could use the train to knock him into the pit of alligators and put some piranhas in there for good measure that….

Wait a minute. It has been more than five minutes and Mr. Bareass is not down here yet. His inability to tell time is just another thing I am going to add to his rapidly growing list of flaws. I dial the room, knowing he's going to pick up the phone.

"Hello."

"Sir, I need you to leave that room. The maintenance people are going to have to get in there. You need to get your stuff and come down to the front desk."

"The maintenance guy is already here. He won't let me take a shower."

Okay. He has got to have some form of mental retardation. I refuse to believe that anyone can be this stupid.

"Dude, you can't take a shower in the room. Haven't you caused enough damage? How much more do you need to cause before your mission is complete?"

"But…"

"Just get out of the room. We will figure something out once you get down here, but you cannot stay in there for another minute."

I slam the phone down before he can come up with another excuse about why he has to shower right this minute. Really, I would like to him to stay up there and shower because I am not in any kind of rush to smell him again, but I don't think a week's worth of showers would get rid of that smell.

"How are things going up here?"

I look up to see Doogie standing in front of me with a smirk on his face. Is it seven o'clock already? Am I really free of this mess? And judging from that fucking smirk, Doogie has absolutely no idea what he just walked into, which brings joy to my heart. I can't help but start laughing in his face.

Doogie isn't quite sure what to make of this because this isn't the first time I've laughed in his face. I can see his mental gear trying to turn to find what I could possibly be making fun of him for this time. There really are so many things, even I can't be sure anymore.

But what I am sure of is that it is seven o'clock and no longer my responsibility. So I look at Doogie and chant in my best fifth grader voice, "A Silver Club member shit in a room. A Silver Club member shit in a room."

And that is how I am going to end this awful day at work. Okay, not really. I am actually going to take my register and skip to the back office singing, "A Silver Club member shit in a room" over and over again.

As I am leaving the hotel for the day, I can see Doogie at the front desk and he has clearly been filled in on what happened up on the thirtieth floor. And because I am that level of mature, I skip by the front desk again. "A Silver Club member shit in a room." Then I laugh all the way to my car.

***

For exactly twelve seconds I felt bad for ditching Doogie with this problem, especially when I realized that Aden ran out of there five minutes after I did. But then I realized I hate him, and I just laughed some more.

Though I did not get out of all of this unscathed. When I got here tonight, I started filling out incident reports and two hours later I am still not finished. I have to write down what I saw over and over again. Because so many things were damaged, I have to fill out a report for each one. The carpet. The wall. The bed. And as it turns out, four other suites surrounding Mr. Bareass's. This is enough to make me hate every single Silver Club member for the rest of time. (Not like I didn't already.)

The final report that was turned in from the maintenance department said that they filled up the wet vac three times getting all the water up from the floors. That's pretty bad since the wet vac can hold up to fifty five gallons of water. That's one hundred and sixty five gallons of water just having a kick ass good time in our hotel. (And how I wish I was exaggerating here.)

A part of me does regret not staying this morning. That's the part of me that really wanted to hear Mr. Bareass trying to explain why he shouldn't have to pay for all of the damage. (Apparently a towel shoved in the drain is a plumbing problem.) The temper tantrum he threw when he found out that they authorized his credit card for $3000, just in case, would have been worth a couple hours less sleep so I could watch it.

But the final total that they decided to charge him was $2500. This total was way too low, in my opinion, but my repeated objections were ignored. I think inflicting that smell on other people should have been well worth $3000. But since no one else's nasal passages were nearly burned off, they don't know the pain.

What's even better is that Mr. Bareass is still here. He actually had the nerve to be pissed off because Doogie moved him to a tiny room on the smoking floor. He felt that, being a Silver Club member, he should still be given a suite. Doogie pointed out that since he had effectively destroyed thirty percent of the suites in the hotel he was pretty much out of luck. Granted, I would have kicked him out on his disgusting ass, but I am still giving Doogie points for being a little bitchy. Which is quite an accomplishment because he usually has his head lodged up the Silver Club members' asses.

All I'm saying is Mr. Bareass better not ask me for a wake up call. If he does, he's going to get a lot more than that. And isn't it enough that I am already going to make fun of him on the internet?

Drinking The Kool-Aid

A Surprising Letter From A Guest

Sean,

I just wanted to thank you for everything you did for me during my stay. I can't tell you how wonderful it is to know that when I stay in your hotel, I will be taken care of. I think it is great how when I arrived you had already had the refrigerator that I requested in the room. I do a lot of traveling for work and stay in a lot of hotels, but I have never felt so taken care of as I was when I stayed with you. I want to thank you very much for going above and beyond your job to make an old lady feel good when staying away from home.

Ms. Leona Akin

(This is an actual letter from a guest. I nearly shit on myself when I read it.)

***

Something very strange is going on. I am not really sure how to handle it. In all the years that I have been working, I have never encountered something like this. I am sure this is one of the many signs of the apocalypse that I know is brewing around the corner.

I am actually being nice to the guests.

Don't get me wrong, I'm still hating them in my mind. I am most definitely still making fun of them behind their backs and making mean comments on the internet, but to their faces, I am actually being quite pleasant. And I don't like it one little bit. It's actually scaring me a little.

So far I have not given attitude to seven different guests who very much deserved a healthy dose. You know, I am sorry that the towels in the hotel are not the same as the ones you have at home, but there isn't a whole lot I can do about that. If you really want towels like the ones you have at home, bring those with you. But I didn't tell them that. You know what I did. I brought them new towels. Granted they were the same as the ones that were already in the room, but I still did it.

And then there was the woman who bitched and moaned because it was too hot in her room, so much that I actually went up to her room to check it out, where she complained until I wanted to jump out the window. Then

284

come to find out the only reason it was hot was because she never bothered to touch her thermostat and the air conditioner was never turned on. Do you know what I told her? "How dare you bother me with this shit when you are too stupid to figure out how to use an on switch!" No. That's not what I said at all. My exact words were, "I'm really glad that I could help you."

I think the Bitchy Committee is meeting right now and is discussing revoking my bitch card.

The fact that the lobby is full of drunk assholes who have decided to throw a massive frat party isn't even making me lose my cool. On the inside I am picturing each and every one of their deaths, but on the outside I am just standing here with a smile plastered on my face. It's freaking Jessie out.

"It just doesn't look natural. It almost looks evil." Gee, I wonder why I don't smile more if this is the reaction it gets.

"Excuse me." A rather unfortunate looking woman is standing at the desk. I can tell just by looking at her that she is not with this group of demon spawn, so I hate her just a little less. "I'm really sorry to bother you because I can see you have enough going on, but I was really hoping you could help me. My room is on the ninth floor and there is a group of these guys hanging out all down the hallways. It's extremely loud. Is there any possible way that I could change rooms to somewhere a little quieter?"

This is usually the point where I go postal all over this woman for wasting my time (which is apparently valuable for some reason that I have not yet discovered), but I just can't do it. First of all, these wannabe frat boys are working my nerves, so I understand where she is coming from. And second, she asked so nicely, which is something no one ever does. "Let me see what I can do."

With just a little work, I find a room on the eighteenth floor that is empty because of a cancellation. I have no idea what the asshole situation is up there, but I am hoping it is a little better than what she is dealing with right now.

After she leaves, I go back to standing at the end of the desk with a fake smile. The only thing that is keeping me alive at this point is my evil thoughts of how these donkeys could die. If only there was some way that I could fill the entire lobby with beer and drown them. But I can't swim so that wouldn't work at all. Perhaps I could...

"Excuse me." The lady who took two seconds out of her life to be polite (See, people, it isn't that hard.) is back. "I am so sorry to come back here. The noise is so much worse on that floor. I just need to get some sleep tonight. I have a very important audition with the symphony in the morning. I flew all the way from Canada for this."

What is this woman doing to me? Not only is she asking for a second room change in twenty minutes, but she just admitted she's from Canada. This is all the reason that I need to hate her. And yet, I just can't do it.

"I'm really sorry, ma'am, but the only reason we had that room is because someone cancelled. All of the other rooms are booked up for tonight."

"Then is it possible to move back to my old room. The noise was loud but not as bad as it is in the second one. I hate to ask."

Holy fuck! If this woman doesn't start screaming about some sort of injustice that she is being forced to endure, I am going to begin to think something is terribly wrong with the world. This woman is not real. It is going to take so little to please her.

"Sure. I'm sorry that I can't do more. I just don't have anything else available at the moment."

"It's okay. I understand. I really appreciate you helping me as much as you have."

This woman is making me hate these people, and this party that is clearly a failed attempt to regain their misspent youth, so much more. She's asking for so little and these bastards can't even let her get some sleep. What's even worse is they are making me be understanding and compassionate towards another human being, and that's just against the Bitchy Committee charter. They are so going to pull my card now.

This is what I get to focus on for the rest of the night. There is some serious mental defect going on inside of me. That is the only explanation for what is going on. That woman was rather annoying. Asking for a room change was crime enough because it made me actually have to do unnecessary work. Asking for a second one should have condemned her to hell. And yet it didn't. Not only did I not use my powers of evil to smite her, I didn't even think about it.

These past couple of weeks that I have been having the uncontrollable urge to be nice to the guests, it has merely been a superficial change. No matter what, I have still been able to think evil thoughts about them. But I couldn't even think of one single bad thing to think about that woman. I even felt bad for her. This is not what I am accustomed to.

I wonder if The Hotel might have been built on top of an old Indian burial ground. (I swear if that little blond girl from Poltergeist shows up, staring at my TV, I am going to go ape shit all over someone.) I mean that has to be the explanation. Or something along those lines. Because the reason can't possibly be that I am becoming a good employee. That's just crazy, right?

Right?

The weirdest thing happened when I came in tonight. With the frat douchebags gone, I figured tonight would be a halfway decent night and, to be honest, what I found when I got here made it just a little bit better.

> I just wanted to thank you again for
> helping me last night. Even with the noise,
> my stay was great. And thanks to you, I did
> really well at my audition. You are very
> helpful.
>
> Carol Chisolm

Attached to this note is a huge chocolate bar. If this woman is not careful she may have me rethinking my hatred for Canadians. (Not really. I am willing to concede that there are a few acceptable ones, but I am sticking to my guns on this one.)

I have never had a guest give me a gift before. Granted, I have been given a couple tips but that's because I actually hauled stuff upstairs for those people. This woman gave me something for doing what, I hate to admit, is my job. And it is actually really nice.

So in the spirit of which it was given, I have decided to spread the love with my co-workers. Well, except for Doogie because he doesn't deserve any chocolate joy. And Leslie doesn't get any either because she is evil. (My new nice attitude does not extend to those two.) So, basically, it is a nice little treat for me and Aden.

And it is, by far, the worst tasting piece of crap ever to wrap itself in foil and call itself chocolate. Aden has to control herself so she doesn't gag. I can't believe there are people in this world who think that this is good. It might be some special form of chocolate for people without taste buds. Though it does make me reconsider offering some to the Dipshitic Duo.

Now, even after this woman may or may not have tried to poison me with this disgusting chocolate bar, I still feel no ill will towards her. No matter how gross, her gesture threatens to melt the ice block that resides where my heart should be.

This cannot possibly be good.

***

I think there might be something to this being nice to the guests thing. Ever since I started doing this, I have been finding that I am not as mean to all people. Maybe all those touchy feely people have been right all along. If you surround yourself with positive energy, you attract more positive energy. I know, right? Vomit. (Maybe my energy isn't quite positive enough.)

But I will have to admit that whatever has been happening to me lately has really boosted my Karma points. All I have to do to find evidence of that is to read the memo that was posted in the back office when I came in tonight.

Doogie is being transferred. I don't think it has quite sunken in yet because I am not standing on the desk doing a white boy dance, but there is definitely a bounce in my step. I don't think I am have been this happy since I found out Lance Bass broke up with his boyfriend.

And it just gets better because he is being transferred to the Housekeeping department. This is funny to me because 98% of the department can't speak English and Doogie can say like three whole words in Spanish. I really wish I could set up a camera in the Housekeeping office just to watch him fall on his butt shaped head.

I can't even think about it without giggling. My facial muscles are working overtime being in the smiling position, which goes against their very nature. This is like a dream come true. I don't think there are words that can do a good job at capturing the amount of joy that I am feeling. The closest I can come to describing it is imagining an all-you-can-eat buffet that only serves fried stuff covered in cheese. And even that doesn't do it justice.

And just to add some sprinkles on the cupcake that is this day, Doogie actually thinks this is a promotion. He doesn't get a change in title (Assistant Manager of Nothing) or a pay raise, so I don't know how he figures that this is a promotion. But he does. And it brings me joy.

I've been thinking about introducing the idea of throwing a Good Riddance party for him, but I am not sure how well that will go over with everyone else. I know Aden would be down for it, but what kind of party is that? Just me and her talking shit about Doogie? It would be just like a regular night at work, except with cake.

I am already scheming different ways that I can give him shit. Being in the Housekeeping department, it won't be hard to come up with something. Many of the people there are cursed with not only a lack of English skills, but with zero IQs as well. For a while, a great deal of them didn't get the fact that if they left dirty room service dishes sitting on the desk, then the room was not completely clean. This is not something I like to find when a particularly pissed off guest insists that I come up to the room to see this myself. I can't even get angry with the person when they are right. (I do not enjoy being deprived of angry thoughts.)

But maybe I shouldn't plot against him. I mean, Doogie is going to have enough trouble without me making it worse. If Doogie thought he had problems with the front desk workers, then he has no idea what he's getting himself into. The housekeepers are going to eat him alive. Not only are they going to hate him and talk massive amounts of shit about him, but they have the advantage of doing it in a language that he won't understand.

Screw it. I am so bringing a cake to work tomorrow and Aden and I are going to go to town.

Maybe if I keep this being nice thing up, Karma will reward me even further and Leslie will win a one way ticket to Loompa Land from that easy listening radio station that she is always inflicting on us in the back office. (Seriously, I am going to kill myself if I have to count down my register while listening to 'I Said I Loved You, But I Lied' one more time. Michael Bolton blows.)

***

I have gotten three more letters from guests thanking me for being so helpful during their stay. I have them all tacked up on my wall as reminders of what being nice gets me. This happens after I wave it in front of the managers' faces to prove that I don't always have a bad attitude and am, in fact, better than them. Okay, I only do that to Leslie.

Things have been going so much better since Doogie has left us. I have given up on my original plan of not plotting against him. Last night, I checked a woman into a room only for her to come back down to tell me that the room was extremely dirty. I checked her into a new room, but curiosity got the better of me, and I had to go check out the room myself. Sure enough, the room was a fucking mess.

This happens because the housekeepers, for some reason, skip that room while cleaning but still mark it as clean in the computer system. This pisses me off because the guests don't really think that far and would just prefer to think that I am a moron for putting them in a dirty room. This angers me. So to exact my revenge, I took pictures of the mess (I love my camera phone.) and had Aden attach them to a strongly worded e-mail to Doogie. This e-mail may or may not have also been sent to all the head of the departments just to show them what an incompetent donkey Doogie is. (That really didn't make us better friends.)

I'm still feeling very smug about my small victories of the past couple of weeks and not even Leslie is going to bring me down, even though it is past midnight and she was supposed to go home over an hour ago, but hasn't, because she has "important work" to do. Apparently this work is to try to irritate me. But she won't get to me that easily. I'm enjoying having Karma on my side for once.

"Excuse me, can I speak to your manager?"

Nothing good has ever come from someone asking that, especially when it comes to me. But I have been so good lately, especially to the woman asking to talk to the manager. She was really nice when she checked in and I hauled her thousand pound bag upstairs for her. I didn't even judge her for traveling with her own personal supply of bowling balls. (What else could have been in that bag? No one needs a bag that full for a one night stay.)

"Um...sure. Is there something..."

Like a fucking jackal that smells blood, Leslie is on top of me before I can even finish my sentence. "I'm the manager. What can I assist you with?"

Dammit. If I have to get a complaint from an ungrateful guest, Leslie is not the person I want to hear it. She is going to try to be all manageresque and give me a lecture on my attitude and then I am going to have to shove a Wonka bar up her ass. I'm just dreading the police report on that one.

"Yes. I'm sorry to interrupt you, but I really just wanted to take a moment to tell you what a wonderful job this young man is doing."

I think I may be having a stroke. This woman isn't here to complain, she's here to compliment me. That has never happened to me. Ever. Sure I got those little notes, but no one has ever gone out of their way to hunt down a manager to tell them I'm doing a good job. And the fact that Leslie has to hear it makes it like a hug from baby Jesus.

"Excuse me?"

The woman looks at Leslie like she is retarded and instantly becomes my favorite person in the whole world.

"This young man," She gestures towards me in a way that tells me she really thinks Leslie is a little slow in the head, "is doing a wonderful job. He is really helpful. He brought my heavy luggage all the way to the twenty seventh floor for me, and he didn't even complain when I didn't have any money to tip him."

"Well, he doesn't work for tips. And if he asked for one…"

"No, he didn't ask for one. But he is clearly not a bellman, so him doing that for me was going beyond his duties. I just thought it should be pointed out, and he should be commended for doing such a great job."

It is clear that Leslie has no idea how to process this information. She can't be rude to the guest, but at the same time she doesn't want to acknowledge that I am doing a good job. That would go against everything she knows. "Thank you, ma'am."

The lady walks away from the desk and I send every happy thought I can muster towards her. For the first time in my life, I want good things to happen to another human being. It's a strange feeling.

It takes Leslie a whole minute to turn around to face me. By this time, I am biting my lip to keep from laughing in her face. She has to be dying right now. Not only does she have to tell me that I did a good job, but she will also have to tell everyone else. This has got to be eating away at her tiny, black soul.

But I save her from having to speak. "What do you know? I'm kind of awesome." I manage to get this out without laughing, which is somewhat of a miracle.

Leslie doesn't say anything. She just walks away towards the office, leaving me alone at the desk to do a victory dance. It only gets better when I hear the door to the office slam shut.

A minute later, I see the lady walking out of the lobby store back towards the elevators. I can't help myself, waving her back over to the desk. "You have just made my whole year." I hand her a free breakfast coupon. And not that shitty breakfast where all you get is soggy generic cereal. No, this woman gets bacon. It's the least I can do for her, seeing as how she broke Leslie's spirit.

"Is it true that you basically carried a drunk guest to his room?"

What does it say about me that the first thing I do is rack my brain to come up with a cover story for any possible wrong doing that may have occurred in this incident? In my defense, when you have Leeland standing over you with that look on his face, you tend to take mental inventory of everything you have ever done wrong in your life. It's always good to have a confession or alibi ready at a moment's notice.

"Um…yes."

It is not likely I will forget that drunk asshole within my lifetime. It had started out as a rather simple night. It was only somewhat busy and I was in a surprisingly good mood. I think I was still living off the high from that guest complimenting me in front of Leslie. But that all changed when the phone rang.

"Hey. This is Marcus from the Really Expensive, Overly Pretentious Hotel down the road from you. (Obviously the name has been changed to protect the innocent. Not really, I just don't feel like being sued.) We have one of your guests over here at our bar." That must be a real treat for him. Why exactly did he call me? Do they lojack all of their guests over there and he assumes

298

we do the same and suspects that this guest's might be malfunctioning. "It seems he has had a little too much to drink tonight. We have already called a cab to take him to your hotel, but we want to make sure that someone will be able to help him when he gets there."

Fucking terrific. Just because I have taken on this new nice to the guests attitude, that does not mean that I have not reserved the right to mentally judge them for the stupid shit they do that impedes on my night. While, yes, technically I am not doing a damn thing. That does not mean that I feel like babysitting some drunken douche nozzle.

"Just send him over and we will take care of him." I know this is true because no matter how much I don't want to or how stupid I think it is, he is a guest with us, and I have to do whatever I can to help him out. (I just know Louise is somewhere, shitting on herself that at least one person is actually doing what she taught us to do in orientation. And since she is a robot, she is being alerted to this behavior at this very moment.)

The next ten minutes are spent mentally preparing myself for what is about to happen. I have never had to assist a drunk person through the hotel before, so I have no idea what to expect. Most drunks are at least able to function enough to get to the elevators, past that point, I no longer care. Who am I kidding, I stop caring long before that. All I do know, for sure, is that if this mother fucker pukes on my shit brown uniform, there will be hell to pay.

The cab finally pulls up to the entrance and I leave Aden at the desk to get this over with. Before I even reach the door, I can see Mr. Drunk Ass has gone way past a little too much to drink. This is proven by the fact that he just did a face plant straight from the cab to the driveway. Nice.

I go outside and help him off the ground because apparently that is outside the scope of the six dollar fare and the cab driver is having none of that. Not that I can blame him because this guy smells straight up ass. If I was stuck in a cab with him for five whole minutes I probably would have driven off while he was still on the ground too.

Getting him inside the hotel is no easy feat. According to the numerous complaints that I have received from drunk guests, the doors are very hard to find. (As well as the thirty story elevators. I have been told that I moved them just to mess with one person.) Now with a drunk person who has lost all control over his legs, finding the doors can be exponentially harder. Not to mention getting through them. I don't even feel bad that Mr. Drunk Ass hit himself in the head with the door twice because he has no fucking clue what is going on.

Clearly, this guy is not going to be able to get to his room under his own power. So like the good front desk person I am, who has the proper attitude for the position that I hold (Suck it, Leslie.), I decide to help him to his room.

"Sir, what is your room number?"

"I don'ts fushcking know. Is up theres." He points randomly up. Helpful.

"Let's try an easier question. What's your name?" This question is surprisingly harder than I had hoped, but armed with his name, I lead him to the front desk. Propping him up, I hope for the best. "Stay right here and I will get a key for your room."

I try to do this as fast as possible because I would really like to be done with this chore. As it is, I will probably never get the smell of cheap beer and regret out of my clothes. It takes me about five seconds to make a key for his room, but in that time Mr. Drunk Ass has completely disappeared.

Aden is helping a woman who has a very scared look on her face like she is afraid that any minutes a homeless person is going to ask her for change.

"Did you see where he went?" Like there is any doubt as to who I am talking about.

Scared Lady doesn't even say anything, just points to the ground. Leaning over the desk, I see him. Mr. Drunk

301

Ass is sprawled out on the floor like he is getting ready to take a nap. Part of me is actually considering getting him a pillow and just leaving him there. In the long run, it would be so much easier.

But I don't. Because honestly, I am kind of feeling bad for this guy. His night is obviously not going the way he planned. He has had way too much to drink, in what I am sure is an obvious attempt to hook up with some woman who never had any intention of sleeping with him. Then he's got to be helped out by me, which I am quite positive is not his ideal of whom he would like to be going to his room with. And now he is making out with the ugly as shit carpet in the hotel lobby. (And whatever germs that might entail.) Seriously, how do you not feel bad for that?

Hauling him back up to his unsteady feet, I let him lean on me because I don't want to risk him falling down again and taking me with him. (I really have no desire to make out with the carpet. That might be his thing for all I know. Not so much mine.)

The elevator is not fun. I only thought he smelled bad out in the lobby. That was before all that smell was contained in a little box. In the elevator, the smell has nowhere to go. It also does not help that I am being used as a support structure for the man out of whose pores the smell is coming. I am picturing myself in a couple hours kneeling beside my bathtub, tears streaming down my face, scrubbing my uniform with industrial strength solvent because a regular washing would just not be enough.

When we get to his floor, I have given up on him actually assisting in the walking process and am just basically dragging him across the floor. (It's not like he is not intimately acquainted with floor already.) I do so hope that tomorrow when his hangover is making him want to die, and he will have one, he rethinks his policy on alcohol.

After what can only be described as a Herculean effort, I get the door opened and him in his room. I suddenly have new respect for those guys you see on TV who are trying to get their motel room door open while a drunk hooker is clinging to him like her kids were to her when they were being taken away by CPS. It is not easy to do.

Inside he falls face first on the bed. I consider this safely deposited in his room and my job done.

"Waisht, youSh need tips."

Oh dear. While I admit that tips are always appreciated and I would never under normal circumstances turn one down AND that I fully deserve one for the effort that I just put forth, I really don't want to stay with him long enough to get one.

"Do you have any money, sir?" Why am I even asking?

"Yesh. My's money thing in my's backsh pockets. Take monies." This man is the worst drunk ever. I have been fucked up drunk before and I still know that my wallet stays in my back pocket. Never once have I told someone to reach in and grab money.

I am actually considering going for the wallet. I won't lie. Yes, technically that would make me a mugger, but I totally have permission. And yes, he might not remember that he gave me permission in the morning, but I will be long gone by then, so what do I care? But also, getting a tip would mean having to get really close to his ass and that smell again. And I guess, you know, I would feel bad if I actually robbed one the guests.

"Yous is kina cutes. Yoush cans stay."

Got. To. Go. NOW. I don't know if he was actually talking to me or imagining some eighteen year old hooker, and I think it is best for my sanity if I never know. The answer would probably bring an unhealthy combination of tears, bathing, and therapy.

I think he's trying to say something else but the door is already closing as I run far, far away.

That guy is going to be burned into my memory until the day I die. My gravestone will probably read "Here Lies Sean. He Helped The Drunk Guy." Not exactly the way I want to be remembered but I guess it beats "Here Lies Sean. He Bitched."

"That was some very good customer service." (Great. Another thing that I don't really want to be known for after my death.)

Leeland snaps me out of my mental reliving of The Night That Shall Not Be Spoken Of. "Well, that is what you pay me for, isn't it?" Why with the smart assiness all the time? Leeland can destroy me with a snap of his fingers. Why do I insist on making comments like this to him?

"And did you complain while doing it?"

"Not verbally." (But mentally it was pretty incessant.)

"Then that is your first step into becoming a manger." Maybe I shouldn't be too worried about making such smart ass remarks in front of Leeland so much because he obviously knows how to use them himself. Me. Manager. Next thing he's going to tell me is that Leslie and I are going to have a picnic together. (And unless I am throwing homemade fried chicken at her, it's not happening.) "You know Aden is planning on moving to Austin soon. There will be a position open. You might want to consider applying for it."

Holy shit. He's serious.

Death By Mermaid

A Letter Addressed To Evil

Dear Leslie,

Suck it, you little fartpincher. You know all that bitching you do about my attitude, well guess what? You can blow it right out of your ass, along with YOUR attitude. Do not get all pissy with me because Leeland likes me better than you. (You should be used to it by now. Everyone likes everyone else better than you.) And under no circumstances are you allowed to tell Leeland that you don't think I would make a good manager, so he shouldn't even consider me.

Oh what? You didn't think I was going to find out. You forget that no one likes you and people are waiting for half an opportunity to rat your ass out.

You are still just pissed off because you had to address that customer compliment on me. Don't think I didn't notice how you were practically gagging the whole time we were talking to Leeland. And I hope it didn't escape your attention that I was practically melting with joy over it.

You need to get over it. Because here's the thing. If I do get the promotion, I will no longer be your employee. We will be equals. And you know what? I know that just CHAPS YOUR ASS. And don't think I won't flaunt it every chance I get. I will be up in your face 24/7.

So here's what I am going to do for you. I am giving you fair warning. If you try to sabotage me again with your comments like "He's not professional" or "He has an attitude problem" or "He refuses to smell my farts and tell me that they smell like roses", I am going to unleash the herd of very hungry Vermicious Knids that I have in my back yard.

I don't care if it will be considered a hate crime. Just call me Loompaphobic.

Sean

P.S. The fact that this letter exists proves that you are probably right about me.

***

There have been a lot of groups and conventions that have stayed with us. Many of them have unleashed anger and mockery from me like no other person has even been able to do before. And yet none of them have even come close to preparing me for the group that arrived tonight.

I never knew that there was an annual convention for romance writers and, quite frankly, I am very happy that I never possessed this knowledge. It just bugs me that there is a convention for just about everything. I just think that it is terribly unfair that all these conventions exist and I don't have one of my very own. It is a travesty of nature that there is not a convention for the disgruntled and the bitchy and the bitter.

I should really consider starting one. It could be called the National Fuck It Convention. We would be an all-inclusive club, except for, you know, people we don't like. Every year we could get together and have a week's worth of classes such as "Vajayjay Flashers and How To Stop Them" or "Getting Rid Of All Traces Of Emotion: Becoming The Next Katie Holmes".

The best part is we could totally fight with the government, claiming we should be tax exempt because we should be considered a charitable organization. I firmly believe that pointing out people's flaws is charity. How else are they going to better themselves if they just spend their whole life thinking that nothing is wrong. (Because we here at the NFIC care enough to tell you the very worst.)

But, I digress.

For the past couple of days the Hotel has been playing host to this romance writers' convention. Basically this is just an excuse for a bunch of horny, middle aged, unattractive women who write trashy romance novels to get together, dress up in clothes that they have no business wearing, and play with sex toys. And this is all done under the guise of a book writers/lover convention.

Under normal circumstance I would be okay with this. I love books. I'm a writer. But we aren't even talking about good trashy romance novels. We're talking full on fucked up trashy romance novels. Like Egyptian God descending from the sky to ravish the poor chained up slave girl fucked up. (Think I'm kidding. I met the woman who wrote it.)

"Excuse me. Where is your bathroom?"

It takes me a few seconds to actually point her in the direction of the bathroom because my retinas have been scorched. The obese woman standing there on the other side of the desk is dressed like a mermaid. A MERMAID! I am talking shiny green material cut to make it look like fish scales. Long tight dress that flares at the bottom. AND

HOLY MOTHER OF GOD, SHE HAS A DORSAL FIN.
Where are the fashion police when you need them?

This isn't the first costume I've seen tonight. This isn't even the worst costume I've seen. The lobby is populated with witches, and flappers, and fairies. And I did not know this but apparently dressing up like a fairy exempts you from having to wear shoes in a hotel lobby. (I hope they enjoyed their foot fungi.)

Far be it for me to judge because in no land could I be considered a skinny waif, but as a big person I know what I can and cannot wear. That is a lesson that many of these women need to learn desperately. If a big girl wants to dress up in a costume, that is fine. But those costumes should not include cleavage revealing serving wench, scantily clad harem girl, or toga wearing Greek goddess. And most certainly not a mermaid. I think it might be a crime against nature to squeeze that much body into so little fabric. It most certainly is a crime against fashion, murdering those poor seams like that.

As my retinas are trying to heal themselves, a loud cackle erupts from a table right next to the bar. A belly dancer, two fairies, and a very drunk slave girl (complete with her own chains) are grouped together in conversation. And they are being none too quiet about it either.

"She should be carried back to their camp where she is tended to and falls in love with Javier." Fairy 1 gestures maniacally when she speaks.

"No. That makes no sense. A horde of hunters would not be compassionate enough to tend to her. The brooding Javier should find the Peruvian hand maiden lying on the bank of the river tending to her twisted ankle and be so overcome with lust that he takes her roughly next to the water." Belly Dancer is scaring me a little at this point.

Slave Girl's contribution to the conversation is a hiccup.

"I don't think I want Javier to take the maiden just yet. They are supposed to fall in love." I don't know how to tell Fairy 2 this, but Javier is gay. He's probably got his eye on that Peruvian whipping boy back home.

You know, I cannot tell you how many times I have had this same conversation with my friends. It seems like every day I am trying to figure out what is to become of the poor Peruvian hand maiden. Peruvian hand maidens are the devil.

I seriously want to go home. I don't know how much more of this I can take. The mockery levels inside of me are boiling over. Pretty soon they are going to come spilling out as uncontrollable word diarrhea. And I cannot, under any circumstances, have that happen. Not when I am trying to look good in front of the managers. The possibility of ever getting a promotion hinges on my ability to keep my mouth shut. (I know. I'm fucking doomed.)

What is helping my case though is that they brought along Playgirl's Man of the Year along with them. He is proving to be quite a useful distraction when it feels like I am about to scream obscenities at the woman who insists on acting out scenes from her latest book in which a modern day New York girl gets whisked away to a magical fairy kingdom where she is seduced by the evil king, has a lesbian encounter with the princess, and finally falls in love with the troll who is actually the good king in disguise. (A copy of this book was left at the front desk, so Aden and I had ourselves a look. It actually made me think about advocating book burnings.) It's a good thing that I have something pretty to look at to keep my mind off the severe gross factor of my surroundings.

The only reason that I haven't gone insane yet is because I know that Leeland is perfectly okay with me mentally hating on these people. It's just the verbal that he's not all about. I totally get that. And honestly, most of my hating is mental anyway. And internetual as well. Yes, there have been some slips and things have escaped my mouth that shouldn't have, but I have been really lucky and not gotten caught on any of them. (Which proves miracles do fucking exist.)

But I have been giving my new outward attitude a lot of thought lately and I keep asking myself why I am doing it? The only answer I have been able to come up with is for the promotion. The truth is I don't really even want the promotion that much. Sure, the extra money would be nice. And the title. And the power that it would give me over other people. But it just seems like a big giant bag of bullshit that I would have to deal with. The beauty of being a lowly agent is that when someone is really pissing me off and I just don't want to deal with it anymore, I can direct them to someone else. As a manager, I would be the person that would deal with it. I think it has been proven already that I don't quite handle being yelled at so well. That could present a problem. Really, the only plus that I can see to even considering the job is because it is making Leslie shit puppies. Which, let's face it, to me, is a huge plus.

And I just know that, no matter what, as a manager I would never be allowed to make fun of the Not So Little Mermaid (God help her if she starts singing Part of Your World) as she waddles across the lobby, be it verbal, mental, or in an internet based forum.

***

It's two o'clock in the afternoon and I am suddenly regretting my decision to make Bon Jovi's "Living on a Prayer" my ringtone. It's not exactly the sound you want jarring you awake when you have been up all night.

"Whhhaaaaaatttt?" I am not the most pleasant person when I have been rudely awoken.

"Sean, this is Leeland."

"Yes, Leeland. You do know what time it is, right?"

"I'm sorry to wake you up, but we have a situation."

And, obviously, it is something that cannot possibly be handled without waking me up from my very much needed sleep. "Okay. What's going on?"

"I can't really talk about it right now." Great. So I am getting a call to tell me that there is some horrible situation happening that he's not allowed to talk about. That makes perfect sense. "I need you to take tonight off and come in tomorrow at ten o'clock for a meeting with HR."

"WHAT?" So all traces of sleepiness are gone. Has being called into HR ever been a good thing? "Why? What's going on?"

"I told you I can't talk about it right now."

"So basically you called me up just to freak me out?"

"I'm sorry. I really am. But I have instructions."

"Am I being fired?"

"Sean, I cannot talk about it. I just need you here at ten o'clock tomorrow. I will see you then."

Fucking terrific.

***

I haven't really slept that much since I got the call
from Leeland. I am not really one of those people who can
get news and not freak the fuck out. So instead of trying to
sleep, I have been racking my brain for why I am getting
summoned to HR. The night has been filled with me
making a very long list of possible incidents that I could
be getting in trouble for. (It was actually a very long list.)

After a frantic call from Stella and Aden, I found out
that they were told nothing about why I was not allowed to
go to work. So with that, I have pretty much resigned
myself to the fact that I am getting fired. If it were
anything less than that, Aden would know something, at
the very least. Also if it were anything else I wouldn't be
going to HR, it would just be some stupid meeting where I
am issued a write up. (It should probably come as no
surprise that, in my working career, I am no stranger to the
write up.)

So it's 9:55 and I am standing outside HR, waiting. I
am trying to come up with multiple defenses for whatever
shit storm I am about to have rain down on me. Since I
have accepted that I am about to get fired, I am trying to
come up with the best way to handle this. On one hand I

315

can do the whole weepy, pitiful thing and beg for my job. Or I could go for righteous indignation, demanding to know why my job is even in question in the first place. At least I have options.

Now that it is exactly 10 o'clock, I can walk into HR and get this bullshit over with. In the office, there is a grumpy looking secretary. And if matters could get any worse right now, Louise is sitting in the corner. She sees me come in and immediately looks away, which is a good thing because I am in no mood for her robotic chirpiness protocols right now. I walk up to the grumpy secretary.

"I have an appointment with someone up here."

The secretary looks up at me with a pissed off look that tells me she wishes I was a bag of Doritos so she could eat me whole. "Yes, you are meeting with Joan." It really doesn't bode well for me that I didn't have to tell her my name for her to know who my meeting is with. "She's not ready yet."

"Well, I was told to show up here at ten o'clock. It's three minutes past. I'd really like to get this done."

"You are just going to have to wait until Joan is ready."

Yeah. This desk jockey is really working my nerves. Granted it is not all her fault because I am a little stressed out, but she isn't helping. "I have been waiting for the past twenty hours. I think that is quite enough, don't you?

I guess it's safe to say that I have decided to go down the righteous indignation path.

Leeland walks through the door so I turn from Grumperella and focus on him. "I'm sorry that I'm late, Sean. Let me talk to Joan for just a second and then we will call you in."

Sure, why not? It's not like I have anything else to do right now. By all means, take your time while you discuss my fate.

I use my time wisely and have a staring contest with Grumperella. I don't exactly get why she's so hostile towards me. She probably knows something that I don't. Which pisses me off. Even secretaries know why I am getting fired before I do. Because that seems fair.

Leeland comes out of this Joan person's office and waves for me to come in. As I walk in I see that Joan is the head of the HR department, which explains why I have never seen or heard of her before. I must be in some serious shit if I am being fired by the department head.

Her office is like a monument to tacky. The walls are brown, which is never a happy color. Shelves are lined with hotel related books. (I never knew so many books were written on a subject so boring.) And the crap decorations makes me want to be physically ill. Clearly, tchotchkes are this woman's friend. Next to her computer is a picture frame of a child who looks like he is trying to figure out a way to strangle himself to get out of taking a picture. Can't say I blame him. If the woman sitting behind the desk was my mother, I would take the easy way out too.

Joan looks like a librarian only more uptight. And she obviously feels that plastic surgery is a waste of money when she can just pull her hair back into such a severe bun that it lifts her whole face.

"Have a seat, Sean." She waves to one of the seats in front of her and I promptly plop my ass down into it. "How are you this morning?"

Is she really going for small talk? Like I am terribly interested in shooting the shit with her after the night I just had because of her. "Sort of freaked out is how I'm doing. I'd really like to know what is going on."

She seems almost disappointed that I want to get right into it. And that's not my problem. If she wants to have a conversation with someone, then she can go buy some friends. I just want to be done with her so I can go back to bed.

"Well, we have come across some very troubling information. Yesterday, we received this e-mail from a guest who stayed here recently. She was very upset and it seems you were the reason."

"And what is it that I did to make her so upset?" It's going to be like pulling teeth to get any information out of her, isn't it? Why exactly does she want to prolong this? Is her life so empty that she has to stretch out this human contact just for something to do?

"She came across an internet posting that she wasn't very happy about."

My blog. I never even considered that as a possibility of why I was being called in here. And really, of all the things that I could have legitimately been brought up here for, my blog is that one that won? Seriously? Literally tens of people read my blog. What are the chances that someone who stayed in the hotel would come across it? Or figure out where I work because I never mentioned the name of the hotel on it. What the fuck?

Now that I know what this is all about, I am freaking out a little less. It's just a stupid blog. (Which I love. And I also love those tens of people who read it.) This is clearly not that big of a deal. They got me all worked up for nothing. I mean it's not like they are really going to fire me over a website.

"Okay, so she wasn't happy about my blog." I don't continue the thought because I cannot see what the big problem is. I am not the only person who says mean things about people on the internet. Perez Hilton has made a career of it. (I hate Perez Hilton. Perez Hilton is the devil.)

"Yes, she is very upset. And rightfully so. Quite frankly, I'm surprised that you would do this."

319

"Surprised? Why?"

"Don't you find it a little bit distasteful? Surely you have to admit that this behavior is very unprofessional." What is it with these people and that fucking word? Unprofessional. It's the first word they grab when anything is wrong. No one can be professional all the damn time. I have even seen Leeland crack under pressure.

"No. I really don't. I complain about my job. Everyone does that."

"Not everyone posts their complaints on the internet. They also don't refer to their guests as "horny, middle aged, unattractive women who write trashy romance novels.""

Fuck. It's those goddamn romance writers. They've been out of the hotel for three days and they are still making my life hell. Obviously, Joan didn't meet these ladies or she would know that my quote is completely accurate.

"No, some people do a lot worse." You know, perhaps being a bitch is not the best course of action at this moment. Maybe I don't want to provoke Joan, seeing as how I have been pulled into a meeting with her. But I can't help it. She's irritating me and I don't really care for it.

"Yes, I'm sure they do, Sean, but they don't work here. Can't you see how this reflects the whole hotel?"

"Not really, since the whole thing is fairly anonymous. I've never mentioned the name of the place on it. So not very many people know where I work."

"This woman did."

"Which is a freak accident. She must have known about it before she got here. Because there is no chance that she just stumbled onto my blog on the same day that I wrote something about her group. That pretty much shows that she didn't have a problem with it before, so why is she complaining now?"

"Probably because she found it rather offensive. I've read through some of the entries you made and I agree with her." Yeah. There's a big shocker. People who dress like librarians rarely find anything amusing. "Sean, because of this, we are going to have to terminate your employment."

"WHAT!?" I shout so loud that I am sure I just scared Grumperella, who is probably choking on a Dorito right now. Not a minute ago, I was sure this was no big deal and they weren't going to fire me over something so stupid. "You're firing me because of my blog?"

"We really don't have much choice, do we?"

"I think you do. One person had a problem with my postings. One person. I have worked my ass off for this

321

hotel. I have come in on my days off. I have worked double shifts. I have done my managers' jobs for them. Now you are telling me that all means nothing because one person complained."

"Sean," Leeland sits up in his chair. He's been so quiet throughout this meeting that I forgot he was there. I would hope that this is the point where he comes to my defense, but I'm sure that is not going to happen. "We are not doing this because of your job performance. You have been a very good employee. So that's not what this is about."

"Yes, the reports that I have received about you have all been very complimentary. That's why I am rather shocked that you would even think about posting these things."

"Why is everyone so shocked that I wrote these things? Everyone knew I was doing it. I even told Paul in my interview for this job that I would be doing this. No one has said anything about it. Why is this all of a sudden a problem?"

"What do you mean everyone knew you were doing it?" Does she need a fucking dictionary? It's probably the only boring book missing from this damn office.

"I mean EVERYONE KNEW. Everyone at the front desk has read them. I used to print them out so they could read them in the office. Leeland has actually been to the website to read them because I said Doogie had a butt shaped head. There was no mention of it being a problem then."

"Is this true, Leeland?"

"Yes. I have been to the website before."

"Why didn't you inform me that this was going on? We could have stopped this before anything happened."

Leeland squirms in his seat a little. It makes me wish I was not getting fired so I could enjoy the fact that this uptight librarian woman is making a big black man act like a child.

"Honestly, I didn't see the issue. I thought it was rather funny."

Thank you. Finally someone is seeing that this is total bullshit and a complete overreaction.

"I'm a little troubled by the fact that this has been going on with your knowledge and you did nothing to stop it. But we will have to talk about that later."

Leeland seems a little relieved that the pressure is off him for a little while. Me, I'm still a little pissed off.

"I still don't understand why I'm being fired for this. One person complained about it." Maybe if I keep repeating it she will finally understand. "Not everyone is going to like it. That's just a fact of life. People get over it." (Not really. I never do. I hold a grudge like a son of a bitch, as will be seen later.)

"Sean, you honestly don't think we could keep you employed here after this, do you? We do have to think about guest safety."

"What? Guest safety? What the hell is that supposed to mean, Joan?" I try to use the same condescending tone that she has been using to say my name, but it just comes across as unabashed hatred.

"After finding these disturbed writings, I don't…"

"Excuse me." All of that righteous indignation that I was feeling earlier comes flooding back into me. "My writing is not disturbed. This is not a manifesto that I have been working on. It's funny. That's why I started the blog in the first place. To be funny."

"I don't find your postings very funny."

"That's because you don't have a sense of humor." Hey, I'm fired and I'm pissed, might as well go for broke. "I don't know where you get off saying that this is a guest safety issue. You act like I have been plotting ways to kill the guests in their sleep. First of all, that's not funny so I have no reason to do that. Second, I am too lazy to do that. All I've done is call them stupid. That's not really the same thing as physical violence."

"The fact that…"

"Are we done? You've already fired me. Is there anything left to talk about?"

"Yes, there is." Joan is straining to keep her voice calm. I'm pretty sure she is doing it to try to keep me calm because she is imagining that I am a psychopath who is going to try to kill her any minute.

"Then get to it. Since I no longer work here, I'd like to leave as soon as possible." Getting fired is kind of freeing. If it weren't for the whole paycheck thing, I would do it every day.

"Sean, I do hope you have learned a valuable lesson." Other than that Joan is fucking bitch, I can't think of one thing that I have learned from this little meeting. "You have been a very good employee here with the exception of this one disturbing incident." If she says disturbing one more time, she will really have a reason to be afraid. Right now, the only safety concern she should be having right now is hers. "If it weren't for this, we would be glad to keep you with us."

"If you are saying this because you think that I am about to go crazy and shoot up the place, you can save your breath. The only thing I want right now is to be gone so I don't have to look at you anymore." I swear I can see Leeland trying to suppress a laugh next to me. That would probably make Joan's bun explode.

"I'd really appreciate it if you controlled your hostility."

"You just fired me. That tends to make me a little hostile. Did you really expect us to sit here and have a tea party after that?" Thing is she probably did. (Sad.)

"Okay, Sean." That sounded a little bit like aggravation in her voice. Such a shame because we were having such a nice conversation. I don't think she quite gets it that I am out to piss her off. "The last thing we need to talk about is the immediate removal of your postings."

I laugh so hard I think I might have spit on her a little. I was totally wrong. Joan does have a sense of humor. Granted, it's not a very good one, but it's there. How else could she come up with such a ridiculous suggestion? When I can finally breath again and I wipe the tears from my eyes, Joan is sitting there with a stern look on her face like she is about to shush me for giggling in the foreign language section.

"You're serious?"

"I most certainly am serious. We would like it to be pulled down by the end of the day."

"Like that all you'd want, lady. That doesn't mean that it's going to happen."

"I'm afraid that we are going to have to insist upon it."

Oh well if she insists. Let me get right on that. "And why would I do that? Out of the goodness of my heart?"

"No, Sean. We would think you would do it because you realize what this has cost you. And we cannot allow you to have writing about the hotel on the internet."

"Let me get this straight. I'm fired, but you still want me to do something for you. I don't think you quite understand what just happened. When you fired me, you took away the only leverage you had over me. I have no obligation to you whatsoever anymore. So no, I won't be taking my blog down. In fact, now that I don't work here anymore, I'm going to start using the name of the hotel."

"I don't think that is a very wise decision."

"You wouldn't. But what are you going to do about it? I am free to say whatever I want, whenever I want, wherever I want. I can't believe you would even think that I would do you the favor of taking down my blog now. What exactly do I owe you? Besides I can't wait to see what the people who read it are going to have to say about you." We fill a few silent moments having a staring contest. It's nice to see that she hates me just as much as I hate her right now. "Now, since we are done. I'm leaving."

"You need to sign your termination papers."

She pushes a paper towards me a little too hard, knocking over one of her butt ugly tchotchkes. I take a pen and draw a line where I am supposed to sign so hard that it rips the paper.

"And you will need to be escorted downstairs to get your register and have it counted."

I take my keys out of my pocket and separate my register key. It shows how pissed off I am because I get it off on the first try. Usually it takes me about an hour and a half to get my keys loose. "Here. Count the drawer yourself." I throw the key on her desk, hitting another hideous trinket. "I'd say it was nice seeing you, but I can't pull that big of a lie out of my ass."

I stand up, giving her one last dirty look before turning around for the door. I almost make a clean break of it too. It would have been nice if Joan hadn't opened her damn mouth. "You are still going to need to be escorted from the property."

I open the door with one hand and wave my other in the air, snapping my fingers. "Then hurry it up! I need to get home so I can post more stuff on the internet!" I say this very loud so that everyone in the HR office can hear me. Really it is still only Louise and Grumperella, but the looks on their faces are priceless. Clearly, these women have founded their own religion around Joan and I am an infidel for speaking to her in such a manner. They can bite me.

I'm walking down the hall very quickly without an escort and I am sure that is making Joan shit on herself. Who knows what kind of horrible things I could be up to if

I am not properly supervised? I might mock some poor bystander who is just standing in the hall minding their own business. In Joan's mind that's the same thing as slicing them up and wearing their skin as a sports coat.

While I am waiting for the elevator, Leeland walks up beside me. "I am supposed to escort you from the hotel."

"I'm sorry for this great injustice dealt upon you."

"Listen, Sean, this wasn't my choice. I had no say in the decision."

"But you didn't fight it, did you?" Did you, France?

Leeland doesn't answer, not that I expected he would. Maybe he's just afraid that I am going to go off on him like I did Joan, which he is completely justified in feeling. The thing about righteous indignation is that it really doesn't go away and it will pretty much lash out at anyone who provokes it in the tiniest bit. Leeland doesn't really want to mess with me right now.

The elevator arrives and we step on. Of course, we are the only ones on it. This is probably going to be the most awkward elevator ride in the history of mankind. When we are shut inside, I stare straight at the metal doors.

"You never did answer my question in there. Why is this all of a sudden a problem when you have had so much warning? Why wasn't this a problem way back in my interview?"

329

Leeland stares straight ahead too. "To some people, this isn't a problem. Others are reacting badly."

"Do you think that I'm a threat to guest safety?"

"No. I think you are pretty funny. But my opinion didn't count for much in this."

"Joan is a bitch."

In the reflection on the doors, I can see Leeland nodding his head a little. I guess he can't really say it out loud. They might think he is a threat to the hotel if he agrees with me.

The elevator opens to the lobby level which is pretty full at the moment. People are sitting around the tables, eating their lunches. Some of the employees move around taking care of business. None of them know that I just got fired and I won't be coming back. It's a little bit sad. Yes, I made fun of most of these people on the internet, but not all of them. Some of them I actually liked. And I am going to miss them.

"If you promise not to shoot up the hotel, I think we can do without the escort."

"I'll see if I can contain myself."

Leeland holds out his hand and I take it. "If you need a reference or anything, you know my number. I am sure this incident won't need to come up."

"Thanks."

I walk away and through the lobby towards the front door. This is not the moment where I take one last look around the hotel and wish that I had done things differently. I don't go up to people and tell them how much I will miss them. I don't let tears fall because I regret having to leave. (The tears will come later when I realize that I can't afford my car.) I just turn and walk out the door.

But on my way out I do swear that if I ever find the bitch who sent that e-mail, I will not rest until I talk shit about her on the internet.

**

The bitch's name is Kelly. It took surprisingly little effort to figure this out. I thought I would have to pull some Veronica Marsian detective skills to figure it out, but it only took like thirty minutes on Myspace.

Here's what I have figured out. There is a list of people who are subscribed to my blog. One of those people was a woman named Kelly. The day that all this happened, Kelly's name disappeared from my subscriber list. So I went and found her profile (which was easy because she forgot to take herself off my friends list) and pulled up her picture. Surprise surprise, I recognize her.

She was one of the bitchy romance writers. She is the one who sent the e-mail.

This is what pisses me off more than anything. This bitch had been reading my blog for months. She thought they were so hilarious. She even sent me messages to tell me how funny she thought they were. But the second that I wrote something about her group (not even her personally) she got all pissy.

If you can't take a joke, then you are not allowed to laugh at other people. I talk a serious amount of shit. I make fun of people left and right. But if someone makes a joke about me, I take it. I know that if I can't take a simple joke, then it makes me a hypocrite when I make fun of other people. (And I am a hypocrite for enough reasons already.)

So, Kelly, fuck you. I hope you live a miserable life alone. And when you die, I hope your twenty-six cats eat your body.

Lessons Learned

Dear Joan,

I think we need to clear a couple things up.
Because, quite frankly, I think you have lost
your motherfucking mind.

Now, we should get this straight. I hate you
and every day I wish for your hotel to get shut
down because you personally somehow
managed to give every single guest in the place
salmonella poisoning. There is no love between
us. And one day, when I have made my fortune
and can live a life of leisure, I will choose to
spend my days throwing eggs at your hotel.

That being said, we need to talk.

I showed up there a couple nights ago to see
Aden and Stella. Now I didn't go inside, and I
am glad I didn't because it was brought to my
attention that I am banned from the property.
Now that does not quite piss me off that much
because I wouldn't step foot inside the place if
Lance Bass was naked and paying me a million
dollars to do it. What does piss me off is that
there are flyers hanging up on almost every

square inch of free wall space with my picture on it, like my very own shitty WANTED poster, saying, "This person is banned from property due to possible actions of a terrorist nature".

Can we just stop for a minute? Acts of a terrorist nature? Are you fucking high?

I would like to know where you get the balls to compare talking shit about people to bombings. I'm not sure how your mind works where you equate calling someone a "horny, middle aged, unattractive woman" with flying a plane into a building. This just proves how fucking stupid you are.

Let me make this very clear to you. I wrote some mean spirited things on the internet. I thought they were funny. That does not make me a terrorist. I did not declare jihad on you. That's a valuable lesson you might want to learn.

So in closing, chill the fuck out. Take some Prozac. Go get a massage. Get laid. I don't really care what you do, but it's obvious you need some help. And while you're at it, do something about that ridiculous bun on your head. People might not hate you so much if you didn't look like a sexually repressed librarian all the time.

Wishing you nothing but pain
and misery in all life has to offer,

Sean

***

This is the part where I am supposed to be all introspective and shit. That's really not going to happen for two very important reasons.

First, I don't do introspection. That would require me to look deep down inside myself and that's just not a pretty sight. And I don't think it would help much to look into the cesspool of bitchy that is my soul. I might just end up getting lost in the dark storm clouds.

And second, I don't see the point. There is no deep psychological reason for what I did. I say mean things about people because I am bitter, plain and simple. I do it because I think it's funny. (Not to mention they made it so easy for me.)

Now don't get me wrong. I am not stupid. I know that I might have been a little harsh. But really, all I did was complain about my job. Everyone does that. It's a part of life. I think part of the reason jobs were created was so people could complain about them. And I may have been a little overdramatic. And mean. And a raving bitch. I get it. (You can stop e-mailing me.) But it's not like I don't openly admit that I am blowing everything out of proportion. Because once again, I think it is funny.

And also, I know that not everyone is going to like what I have to say. (I do keep the e-mails.) But, people like

Joan and Kelly (at least before I talked shit about her people) are not my target audience. If those people come across my blog and don't like it, the best course of action is to not read it. Two great big overreactions don't make a right.

The blog was just for fun. (And still is.) It was just a place for me to make a few jokes. Yes, they were at other people's expense, but the same thing can be said about high school, and I don't see people rushing to shut those down. And some people took it entirely too seriously. But that's okay because I am sure that I will eventually make fun of them too.

I would like to point out that I am well aware of the fact that I should have been fired. But not for the reason I was. I was a pretty decent employee, but I did a lot of covert bitchy shit. That's what I should have gotten fired for. And possibly my disrespectful attitude towards Doogie and Leslie. But come on, not even their mothers care about them.

I will be asked in the near future if I regret starting the blog and I don't even have to think about my answer. No. Not even in the slightest. I will go out on a limb and say that it is the best thing that I have ever done. (Not really, but I am all about the over exaggeration.) Sure, I was fired for doing it, therefore making me question my sanity and threatening my relationship with my car, but it was fun. I

337

got to write, which is all I've ever wanted to do. And people actually read it. And liked it. It's really a step up from having notebooks filled with stuff that no one will ever see.

***

I think I am about to sink into this couch with all its über fluffiness. If it weren't for the awful reason that I am sitting on it, I might actually like it and try to take a nap. That wouldn't really be a change from what has been going on in my life for the past couple of months. My life has just kind of been what happens between naps, which has namely been watching Grey's Anatomy reruns again.

It feels weird to be sitting here in something other than my pajama pants, but those really wouldn't have been appropriate for outside viewing. So I picked out the best clothes that I own and ventured forth into the world again.

Sitting across from me is a woman that I immensely dislike already. She is giving off an aura that talking to me is entirely too far beneath her and she should be sitting back on the fluffy couch being fed grapes or some shit. Yeah, like she's that special.

"So tell me, Sean, why do you think you would do well working for us?" It's very hard to understand what she's asking through her outrageously thick Indian accent, but I get the gist.

"I've been working in the customer service industry for the past eight years and I find that I am very much a people person."

It's a vicious circle, isn't it?

Sean Fox has lived in many places. He graduated from Louisiana State University with a degree in Creative Writing and is now just living down the shame. After bouncing around in retail for many years, he has settled in Houston with a job that he sometimes tolerates. If you are looking for more, please visit Sean at www.lancebassruinedmylife.com.

Made in the USA
San Bernardino, CA
18 August 2014